Vitality
and
Aging

IMPLICATIONS OF THE RECTANGULAR CURVE

James F. Fries
Lawrence M. Crapo

STANFORD UNIVERSITY SCHOOL OF MEDICINE

W. H. FREEMAN AND COMPANY   San Francisco

Project Editor: Larry Olsen

Interior Designer: Ron Newcomber

Cover Designer: Sharon H. Smith

Production Coordinator: Linda Jupiter

Illustration Coordinator: Cheryl Nufer

Compositor: Graphic Typesetting Service

Printer and Binder: The Maple-Vail Book Manufacturing Group

The lines of verse at the beginning of each chapter are from Oliver Wendell Holmes, "The Deacon's Masterpiece; or, The Wonderful 'One-Hoss Shay' " from *The Autocrat of the Breakfast Table* (1857–1858). The lines of verse on page 9 from "Do Not Go Gentle into That Good Night" are from *The Poems of Dylan Thomas.* Copyright 1952 by Dylan Thomas. Reprinted by permission of New Directions and J. M. Dent.

Library of Congress Cataloging in Publication Data

Fries, James F.
    Vitality and aging.

    Bibliography: p.
    Includes index.
    1. Aging.   2. Longevity.   3. Vitality.   I. Crapo,
Lawrence M., 1938–   .   II. Title.
QP86.F73   612'.67   81-4566
ISBN 0-7167-1308-X   AACR2
ISBN 0-7167-1309-8 (pbk.)

2 3 4 5 6 7 8 9 10   MP   0 8 9 8 7 6 5 4 3 2

CONTENTS

PREFACE   ix

THE RECTANGULAR CURVE   xi

CHAPTER ONE

A NEW SYLLOGISM   1

wherein the study of human aging is seen to point
toward unusual conclusions

CHAPTER TWO

THE MYTH OF METHUSELAH   11

wherein tales of extreme longevity are analyzed
and found wanting

CHAPTER THREE

AGING AND THE
RECTANGULAR CURVE   25

wherein the survival curves of people and animals
begin to assume a curious shape

CHAPTER FOUR

THE HAYFLICK LIMIT   43

wherein cells and tissues appear to have
discrete and finite life spans

CHAPTER FIVE

THE ELIMINATION OF
PREMATURE DISEASE   59

wherein a dramatic medical and social success story
is seen to have changed our world

CHAPTER SIX

THE SHARP DOWNSLOPE
OF NATURAL DEATH   69

wherein the end of a natural human life is observed
to be fixed at an average of 85 years, even without disease

CHAPTER SEVEN

THE EMERGENCE OF
CHRONIC, UNIVERSAL DISEASE   79

wherein the diseases of aging and of the aged
are seen to be the major challenges of human health

CHAPTER EIGHT

NATURAL LIFE
AND NATURAL DEATH   97

wherein it is indicated that the diseases of aging
may be postponed by personal decisions

CHAPTER NINE

THE PLASTICITY
OF AGING   107

wherein the major manifestations of senescence
are shown to be modifiable

CHAPTER TEN

TRIUMPH AND DESPAIR   123

wherein the burden of personal choice
is observed to present an existential conflict

CHAPTER ELEVEN

THE ONE-HOSS SHAY   135

wherein a vigorous adulthood with a terminal collapse
is seen as a celebration of life

APPENDIX A

LIFE TABLES   143

APPENDIX B

GOMPERTZ'S LAW   147

APPENDIX C

THE STREHLER–MILDVAN
THEORY OF AGING   151

REFERENCES   153

INDEX   167

PREFACE

From many disciplines, studies of human aging point us toward a future that few have anticipated and for which our belief structures, our science, and our society are not well prepared. The central observation is that patterns of aging may be altered but that the average life span is fixed. The increasing period of vitality thus converges with a fixed duration of life. The form of the human survival curve is becoming ever more rectangular. This book is about the implications of this shift in the geometry of our actuarial data for our future as individuals and as a society.

The concepts of aging developed in this book have their roots in the careful work of many investigators. We are particularly indebted to Paul Baltes, Jim Birren, Alex Comfort, Rene Dubos, Caleb Finch, Leonard Hayflick, George Martin, Jack Riley, Matilda Riley, George Sacher, Martin Seligman, Bernard Strehler, Lewis Thomas, and George Valliant, whose writings have greatly influenced our own views of aging and the rectangular society.

In our attempt to be both accurate and clear, we have been greatly aided by critical reviews of all or part of the manuscript by Margret Baltes, Paul Baltes, Melvin Britton, John Bunker, Stephen Coles, Alex Comfort, Kathy Crapo, Philip Crapo, Paul Feigenbaum, Caleb Finch, Sarah Fries, Victor Fuchs, Leonard Hayflick, Henry Hilgard, Halsted Holman, Al Liebman, Elizabeth Loftus, Robert Marcus, Thomas Okarma, Gerald Reaven, Jack Riley, Matilda Riley, David Rogers, Martin Seligman, and George Valliant. We gratefully acknowledge their help and take full responsibility for any remaining confusion or inaccuracy.

Manuscript preparation was marvelously coordinated by Sharon Joseph. Scip Wylbur tirelessly typed and retyped the manuscript. The editorial encouragement of John Staples, Larry Olsen, and the staff at W. H. Freeman and Company has helped immeasurably in making this book a reality.

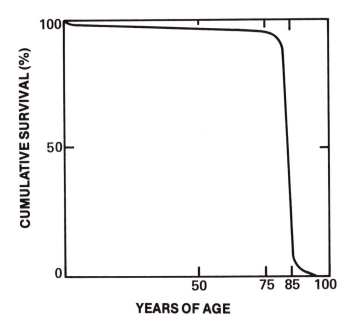

THE RECTANGULAR SURVIVAL CURVE

THE RECTANGULAR
CURVE

Statistics of mortality are often visually displayed as a plot on a graph, called a survival curve. The most common survival curves plot cumulative survival (percentage of the population remaining alive) on the vertical axis and year of age at death on the horizontal axis. For wild animal populations and human populations in hostile, uncivilized environments, the resulting survival curve approximates a simple exponential decay. For such populations, subject to predators, disease, and natural catastrophes, death is a daily reality, and the exponential decay curve implies that death is about as likely to occur at one age as at any other. For civilized human populations, the shape of the survival curve begins to bend upward to the right and to describe a different curve, indicating that most deaths occur at increasingly advanced ages. For our own society, the shape of the survival curve is moving toward that shown in the figure on the opposite page. The initial dip following birth represents infant mortality. Then, the slow decline from age 1 year to about age 70 years demonstrates the small percentage of deaths occurring during those years. After age 75, the curve makes a sharp downward turn, and, after only a few more years, nearly all the members of the population have died. Finally, the curve slackens its descent to represent those few individuals surviving to very old ages. This is the rectangular curve.

Of course, the rectangular curve is not a perfect rectangle. If it were, all deaths in the population would occur at the same age, an occurrence inconsistent with biological statistical distributions. In our society, the shape of the survival curve is becoming increasingly rectangular as more and more individuals survive to advanced ages. As infant mortality declines, as the number of deaths from accident and violence during the middle years of life declines, or as the number of deaths from acute and chronic diseases in the later years of life declines, the survival curve becomes increasingly rectangular. This is the "rectangularization of the survival curve." Given present trends in mortality in the United States, we are on the verge of becoming a "rectangular society" in which nearly all individuals survive to advanced ages and then succumb rather abruptly over a narrow age range centering about age 85.

To understand the implications of the rectangular curve, one must distinguish between two terms, *life span* and *life expectancy*. The life span is the biological limit to length of life. Each species has a characteristic average life span. This life span appears to be a fixed, biological constant of the species. For human beings, the life span has not changed for millennia. Life expectancy refers to the number of years of life expected from birth for an individual or a group. Life expectancy from birth cannot exceed the life span, but it can closely approximate the life span if there is little death at early ages. In contrast to the fixed human life span, life expectancy is increasing rapidly in most countries. Increasing life expectancy is thus on a converging course with the fixed life span represented by the down-slope of the rectangular curve. The following chapters explore the implications of that impending collision.

Vitality
and
Aging

Have you heard of the wonderful one-hoss shay,
That was built in such a logical way
It ran a hundred years to a day,
And then, of a sudden, it—ah, but stay,
I'll tell you what happened without delay,
Scaring the parson into fits,
Frightening people out of their wits,—
Have you ever heard of that, I say?

CHAPTER ONE

A NEW
SYLLOGISM

wherein the study of human aging is seen to point
toward unusual conclusions

Why do we age? Why do we die? How can we live longer? How can we preserve our youth? Questions about life, aging, and death are fundamental to human thought, and human beings have speculated about the answers to these questions for centuries. Our own age values the methods of science—the methods of gathering evidence, of observation, of experiment—above the musings of philosophy. Yet, philosophical speculation and scientific theory may interact and enhance each other. The scientific theories of Copernicus and the conception of a sun-centered solar system, of Newton and an orderly universe, of Einstein and the relationship between matter, energy, and spacetime, of Darwin and the evolution of species have influenced our notions of who we are, where we are, how we came to be here, and the meaning of life itself. Similarly, the study of health and aging may contribute a new philosophical perspective to these age-old questions about life and death.

The implications of new scientific discoveries are often not widely appreciated for many years. Scientific knowledge develops by small increments within a relatively cloistered scientific community, whose members are sometimes more interested in the basic ideas than in their social implications. The increasing sophistication of scientific experiments further obscures our understanding of their meaning, since each new scientific field quickly develops an independent vocabulary and a narrow range of external communication. Public insight into new science often takes the form of controversy—over uses of nuclear power, the hazards of recombinant DNA research, or the contamination of the environment—rather than excitement over new philosophical implications.

So it is with the study of human aging. The ancient philosophical questions have largely fallen to those who search for the biological mechanisms that affect our vitality and that cause our death. The study of aging as a separate scientific discipline is relatively new and is not yet the province of any single science. Independent observations have been made in medicine, in psychology, in molecular biology, in sociology, in anthropology, in actuarial science, and in other fields. There are remarkable parallels in the ideas that have emerged from these independent fields of research. It is our intention to review these parallel developments and to present a synthesis of scientific ideas about human aging that will offer insights into the fundamental questions about the nature and meaning of the life process, aging, and death.

THE INCOMPLETE PARADIGM

The growth of scientific knowledge historically has been impeded by thought systems (paradigms) that worked well for a time but that increasingly failed to explain new observations. For the study of aging, the contemporary paradigm is often called the *medical model*. The medical model defines health as the absence of disease and seeks to improve health by understanding and eradicating disease. This model of life and health, while useful, has obscured a larger perspective.

There are four prevalent beliefs in the medical model that have proved to be limiting (see box at top of page 3). Certainly, few present scholars hold these beliefs literally, but these ideas nonetheless have largely defined contemporary opinion about the aging process.

These four premises seem to imply the following conclusions. If the human life span is increasing, then our scientific goal can be the achievement of immortality. If death results from disease, our objective must be the elimination of disease. If disease is best treated with medication, our strategy is to seek the

---

THE LIMITING PREMISES

1. The human life span is increasing.
2. Death is the result of disease.
3. Disease is best treated by medication.
4. Aging is controlled by the brain and the genes.

---

perfect drug or surgical procedure. With regard to aging, the medical model suggests that we should perform basic research to understand the genetic, neurologic, or hormonal mechanisms that control the process, and then learn to modify them.

Historically, these premises, objectives, and strategies have been useful. They are still worthy and deserving of study and hope. But they are certainly incomplete, and, taken literally, they are misleading. The human life span is not increasing; it has been fixed for a period of at least 100,000 years. The popular misconception of an increasing life span has arisen because the average *life expectancy* has increased; the *life span* appears to be a fixed biological constant. Three terms must be understood. The maximum life potential (MLP) is the age at death of the longest-lived member of the species—for human beings, 115 years. The life span is the age at which the average individual would die if there were no disease or accidents—for human beings, about 85 years and constant for centuries. The life expectancy is the expected age at death of the average individual, granting current mortality rates from disease and accident. In the United States, this age is 73 years and rising.

Death does not require disease or accident. If all disease and all trauma were eliminated, death would still occur, at an average age not much older than at present. If premature death were eliminated, and it may be in large part, we would still face the prospect of a natural death.

Medical treatment is not the best way to approach current national health problems. The major chronic diseases (atherosclerosis, cancer, emphysema, diabetes, osteoarthritis, and cirrhosis) represent the major present health threat. They are deserving of continued medical research, and further advances are to be expected. But abundant evidence points to personal health habits as the main risk factors for these diseases. Preventive approaches now hold far more promise than do therapeutic approaches for improving human health.

Aging does not appear to be under direct control of the central nervous system or the genes. Rather, the aging process occurs in cells and in organs. The aging process is most likely an essential characteristic of biological mechanisms. The process of aging, or *senescence,* is an accumulation in cells and organs of deteriorating functions that begins early in adult life. Aging may result from error-prone biological processes similar to those that have led to the evolution of species.

So the prevailing ideas about aging are incomplete. An increasing body of new scientific information requires revision and extension of these ideas. The time for a new synthesis has arrived, heralded by a number of new discoveries that do not fit well into the old paradigm but that as yet lack a coherent paradigm of their own.

COMPETING THEMES

Changes in our ideas about health and aging are now being reflected in our social institutions and lifestyles. Change in a prevalent system of thought is often turbulent, and such turbulence is now manifest in health by a set of new movements. Within the medical community, there has been increasing recognition of the importance of preventive medical approaches. Such technical strategies as mass screening have been promoted. New departments of preventive medicine have been developed within medical schools; previously, such efforts were largely carried out within schools of public health. These developments are not entirely successful (screening efforts have proved disappointing, and some departments of preventive medicine have not thrived), but their very creation acknowledges the ferment of new approaches to health care.

The public has asked for more active involvement in consumer choices and for more accurate information on which to base such choices. In response, a self-care movement in health has developed, which now represents a considerable social force. At its best, this movement encourages critical consumption of medical services and increased autonomy from professional dominance. At its worst, the self-care movement takes an adversary stance and would replace professional medical treatment with idiosyncratic folk remedies. Still, the growth of these movements indicates discontent with the prevailing medical orthodoxy.

Recent changes in personal lifestyles have been even more significant. Joggers organize footraces in which tens of thousands compete, and cocktail party conversations concern the number of miles run per week. The number of militant antismokers has grown, and the nonbelievers are being packed into smaller and smaller spaces in the back of the airplane. Such spontaneous social changes are very likely to have constructive effects on health, and we applaud them, but the point is that the phenomenon itself represents a profound changing of the public consciousness.

Within professional medicine, new themes are evident. There is an increased interest in long-term patient outcome as a goal and less interest in correcting the trivial laboratory abnormality that does not materially affect the patient. Benefit–cost studies are sometimes advocated as a solution to the astronomical increases in the cost of medical care. Many observers have pointed out that orthodox medical approaches have reached the area of diminishing returns. The quality of life, rather than its duration, has received increasing emphasis.

Both psychologists and physicians have recently described strong relationships between psychological factors and health, and theories explaining such relationships have been developed that emphasize life crises, helplessness, loss of personal autonomy, depression, and other psychological factors. Correction of such psychological problems, it is implied, will improve health, and indeed the circumstantial evidence that this may be true is quite convincing. Again, these approaches are outside the orthodoxy of the medical model.

Two new research areas have recently been emphasized—chronic disease and human aging. Increasingly, researchers recognize the central roles that aging and chronic disease play in our current health problems. The study of aging and of chronic disease is oriented toward long-term outcomes, is interdisciplinary, requires preventive strategies, seeks to demonstrate the relevance of psychological factors, and uses lifestyle modification as a major tactic. The student of aging and the student of the diseases of the aged now have a unique opportunity to harmonize the incomplete old orthodoxy and the emerging new themes.

A NEW SYLLOGISM

Using new knowledge of human aging and of chronic disease, we attempt here to provide a model that harmonizes these competing and chaotic themes, one that points toward new strategies of research and of health attainment. Our theoretical structure allows predictions to be made, and the predictions are strikingly different from those traditionally expected.

Figure 1-1 illustrates some commonly held misconceptions about mortality and aging, drawn in the form of human survival curves, which plot the number

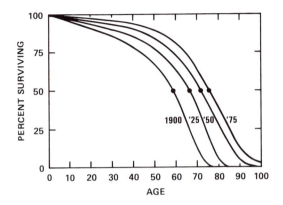

FIGURE 1-1.
Human survival curves. On this graph is plotted the percent of the population that survives to each age for 1900, 1925, 1950, and 1975. However, only the median deaths and the 1950 curve are accurate; the other curves are incorrect and give the false impression that the human life span is increasing. Life expectancy is increasing, as shown by the increase in median age at death. But the true curves are not shifting toward the right in a parallel manner; instead, they are becoming more rectangular, as in Figure 1-2. (National Bureau of Health Statistics.)

of individuals surviving past each year of life. This graph is incorrect! These data do portray accurately the increase in the median age at death over time, and the survival curve for the year 1950 is also accurate, but the other curves are *not* correct. This graph presents a false view; it suggests that individuals are living longer because the maximum life span is increasing.

Of course, no one has ever published such a graph and claimed that the life span is increasing. But, if we ask our students to draw the changes in mortality in this century, they frequently draw a figure similar to Figure 1-1. And, as we shall see in later chapters, much scientific thought and social planning assumes the existence of such curves.

Consider the implications of such a diagram. The number of old people continues to increase without limit. The number of very, very old people will soon be immense. The number of feeble individuals in the population increases with time. The percentage of an individual life spent infirm, frail, or dependent increases. The social requirement for facilities to house the dependent and the resources required to care for them increasingly drain the energies of the still

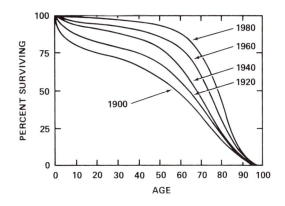

FIGURE 1-2.
Human survival curves for 1900, 1920, 1940, 1960, and 1980. These curves are correct.
They converge at the same maximum age, thereby demonstrating that the maximum
age of survival has been fixed over this period of observation. (National Bureau of
Health Statistics.)

vigorous. The medical-care cost spiral continues to rise. And, in a very real sense,
one may speak of the prolonging of dying rather than the prolonging of life.

Figure 1-2 shows the actual data. Quite opposite and startling conclusions
follow from these data. The number of extremely old persons will not increase.
The percentage of a typical life spent in dependency will decrease. The period
of adult vigor will be prolonged. The need for intensive medical care will decrease. The cost of medical care will decrease, and the quality of life, in a nearly
disease-free society, will be much improved.

Adult life may be conveniently divided into two periods, although the dividing
line is indistinct. First, there is a period of independence and vigor. Second, for
those not dying suddenly or prematurely, there is a period of dependence, diminished capacity, and often lingering disease. This period of infirmity is the
problem; it is feared, by many, more than death itself. The new syllogism does
not offer hope for the indefinite prolongation of life expectancy, but it does point
to a prolongation of vitality and a decrease in the period of diminished capacity.

A NEW SYLLOGISM

1. The human life span is fixed.
2. The age at first infirmity will increase.
3. Therefore the duration of infirmity will decrease.

There are two premises to the syllogism; if they are accepted, then it follows that there will be a reversal of the present trend toward increasing infirmity of our population and increased costs of support of dependency. In the following chapters, we present data from the several fields encompassing the study of human aging; these data support the premises. The first premise is almost certain; the second is very probable. If, after careful evaluation of the supporting data, one accepts the premises of this syllogism, then one must accept the conclusion and the implications of the conclusion.

SOME QUESTIONS OF SEMANTICS

Nuances of meaning may mask the substance of a subject, and slight changes in emphasis may allow a new perspective to be better appreciated. There are problems with several of the terms often used to describe health, medical care, and aging. Among these are *cure, prevention, chronic, premature death,* and *natural death.* We will use these terms in slightly different senses than is usual.

Cure is a term with application to few disease processes other than infections. The major diseases of our time are not likely to be cured, and we have tried to avoid this term. *Prevention* is better but is unfortunately vague; this term, as we shall see, is sometimes misleading. We prefer the term *postponement* with regard to the chronic diseases of human aging, since prevention in the literal sense is difficult or impossible. *Chronic* is a term usually used to denote illnesses that last for a long period of time. It serves as a general but imprecise way of distinguishing the diseases that may be susceptible to cure (such as smallpox) from those better approached by postponement (as with emphysema). Regrettably, this important distinction cannot be based solely on the duration of the illness, since some diseases that last a long time both are not chronic conditions and might eventually be treatable for cure (such as rheumatoid arthritis and ulcerative colitis). We limit our use of the term *chronic* to those conditions that are nearly universal processes, that begin early in adult life, that represent insidious loss of organ function, and that are irreversible. Such diseases (atherosclerosis, emphysema, cancer, diabetes, osteoarthritis, cirrhosis) now dominate human illness in developed countries. We hve defined *premature death* simply as death that occurs before it must, and we have used *natural death* to describe those deaths that occur at the end of the natural life span of the individual.

We bring together in this book the impressive evidence for a biological limit to the human life span, seeing disease in old age as simply an "epiphenomenon," a straw on the back of an already senescent camel. Superficially, some disease always appears to cause death, but the underlying cause in old age is the decrease in defense mechanisms of the organism due to senescence.

THE THEME OF ATTAINABLE LIFE-LONG VITALITY

The theme of attainable life-long vitality represents both our hypothesis and our conclusion. Our syllogism concludes that the period of vitality may be prolonged, and the data suggest the manner by which this end may be achieved. Here is a solution to the fear of a lingering death—in the concept of the natural life. The celebration of the mature years has, of course, been intimated many times before; we are particularly fond of these lines from Browning's "Rabbi Ben Ezra":

> Grow old along with me!
> The best is yet to be,
> The last of life, for which the first was made. . . .

However, along with the strategy for maintaining the vigor of adult life come anguish, pain, and only sometimes triumph. We shall return to this point. Dylan Thomas has anticipated it with these lines:

> Do not go gentle into that good night,
> Old age should burn and rave at close of day;
> Rage, rage against the dying of the light.
>
> • • •
>
> And you, my father, there on the sad height,
> Curse, bless, me now with your fierce tears, I pray.
> Do not go gentle into that good night.
> Rage, rage against the dying of the light.

So the Deacon inquired of the village folk
Where he could find the strongest oak,
That couldn't be split nor bent nor broke,—

CHAPTER TWO

THE MYTH OF
METHUSELAH

wherein tales of extreme longevity are analyzed
and found wanting

Speculation about human longevity and rejuvenation have flourished since antiquity in many different societies. These conjectures are symbolic of a basic desire for a long life and for youth in old age. Because they provide a window through which we may view human potential, we must examine them closely. The methods that a few people have used to preserve vitality and extend life might be the means by which we all could improve our lot. If immortality is possible, those individuals who have come the closest to it deserve careful scrutiny, since they may be anticipating our own future.

A careful look at these speculations, however, reveals them to be composed of various combinations of four myths—the myth of the super-centenarian, the myth of Shangri-La, the myth of Methuselah, and the myth of the Fountain. Although, as with miracle cancer cures, there is no permanent way of ending such myths, the evidence decays rapidly under critical examination. There remain, however, some important conclusions to be drawn about the types of lifestyles that underlie vitality in old age and about the human tendency to prefer quality of life to its quantity and to fear lingering disability more than death.

THE MYTH OF THE SUPER-CENTENARIAN

What is the greatest age ever reached? What is the maximum human life span? Who is the oldest human? Was it Shirali Mislimov of Azerbaijan, USSR, who died in 1973 at a reputed age of 168 years? Or Charlie Smith of the USA, reputed to be 137 years old in 1979? There are many problems with each of the pretenders to the title of world's oldest human. The 1980 *Guinness Book of World Records* accepts as documented only five persons living beyond the age of 112 years, the oldest being Shigechiyo Izumi of Japan, at 114 years of age. Charlie Smith was found to be actually only 104. Mislimov had no written documents of age. Other apparently long life spans have been found to represent grandfather, father, and son with the same name. Age exaggeration seems as prevalent in the very old, particularly in the poorly educated, as is age reduction for the middle aged.

The central problem in the study of longevity is the verification of age. There are no rings on the human tree. There are as yet no reliable biochemical markers that enable one to be certain of the age of a claimant. One cannot use carbon 14 dating to determine the age of a person. And, with many illiterate or semiliterate people, the very concepts of dates and ages are not well developed. Students of the extremely aged deal with such statements as "I was born the year that the great black hunter died in the snowfall" or "My age is between 110 and 140 years." Formal records of births and deaths have been maintained in developed countries for several centuries, but even now such records are scarce in some less-developed lands, and ages reported in censuses are not verified by birth certificates.

Research about claims of great age makes use of all confirming data available—from brothers and sisters, gravestones, baptism certificates, marriage certificates, birth certificates, school classmates, and so on. By estimating age from as many as eleven separate sources, reliable confirmation can be obtained for many people, even in rural or primitive areas. An acceptable objective age estimate can be found for at least three-fourths of the claimants in most areas. We have reviewed studies investigating a total of over 600 super-centenarian candidates. So far, the oldest confirmed age remains 114.

In fact, it can be rather confidently stated that there are no super-centenarians (over age 120) in the Western developed countries. Sweden, England, Wales, and the United States have kept good records since about 1832. Sweden makes a practice of investigating the records of very old individuals carefully. In the Western countries, the oldest documented death is of a Canadian at 113 years, 124 days.

THE MYTH OF SHANGRI-LA

This second myth arises from the ashes of the first. Even though there are no super-centenarians in our society, this myth suggests that there might be small, secluded places in the world where the very, very old live. These cultures might have discovered insights into the true meaning of life. They live without our stresses and our environmental pollutants and our pleasures of the flesh. In purity and in contemplation, they live in distant Shangri-La.

The myth of Shangri-La evolves from the Greek legend of the Hyperboreans, who lived a thousand years, free from all natural ills, in a land of perpetual sunshine beyond the north wind; finally, satiated by their long life of luxury, they leaped into the sea. The Hyperborean theme can be traced through the folklore of many different cultures, including our own. In Hilton's novel *Lost Horizon,* the people of Shangri-La in the Himalayas have prolonged life spans. The present-day myth that extremely old people exist in primitive and mountainous regions of Ecuador, Russia, and Pakistan is a direct descendant of the legend of the Hyperboreans.

Three remote communities have received international attention and scientific pilgrimages in recent years—the district of Abkhazia in the Caucasus Mountains of the USSR, the province of Hunza in the Karakoram Mountains of northwestern Pakistan, and the isolated village of Vilcabamba in the Andes Mountains of Ecuador. The distinguished American physician Alexander Leaf has probed the lifestyles of these communities for a common denominator that might be the secret of longevity. He and others have carefully studied the attributes of some very old people, probably at least 80 to 100 years of age, in what would generally be considered hardship societies—rural, mountainous, high altitude, very low income.

Several important lifestyle patterns are common to the three regions considered to be analogous to Shangri-La. Diets are low in calories and animal fats.

There is a strikingly high level of physical activity and fitness, including active farming and tilling the ground in old age. Obesity is extremely uncommon. There is moderation in alcohol and tobacco consumption. Very importantly, there is no retirement in these communities, and elderly people remain active in social and economic life; a sense of usefulness and purpose pervades the lives of old people in all three cultures. These observations of vigorous, meaningful life in old age are exciting, despite the now unequivocal evidence for age exaggeration in these remote communities.

Many considerations indicate the fallacy of the myth of Shangri-La. We note the close correlation between regional illiteracy and percentage of claimed centenarians in a society. We note the great decrease in the number of black centenarians in the United States as blacks moved from slavery to citizenship. We note the parallel decreases in the USSR as good vital statistics began to be compiled for a region. And we note the absence of any documented area of super-longevity. It is not the belief that some primitive peoples might live long that is illogical so much as the premise that these are the only peoples with that attribute. Sweden holds many of the world health records; why are there not long-lived farmers in rural Sweden? Our innate skepticism about societies with super-centenarians gets a healthy boost from the critical analyses that have been made of such societies.

The most thorough studies have been done in Vilcabamba by Mazess and Forman (1979). They discovered systematic age exaggeration after age 70 and concluded that there was no evidence whatsoever for greatly increased longevity in the Vilcabamba population. There was a higher than usual proportion of Vilcabamba residents over age 60 as compared with the Ecuadorian average, but this seemed to reflect factors (such as migration patterns) other than longevity. The question of lifestyle as another reason for Leaf's observations of extraordinary vigor in old age remains open.

Mazess and Forman's methods were painstaking and thorough. Through a meticulous household census, detailed genealogies for the village inhabitants were constructed. The census, which included 80% of the entire population of 1100 persons in Vilcabamba, also provided the stated ages of the inhabitants. The construction of accurate genealogies was essential because of the frequent duplication of names, which had led to misidentification of individuals in previous studies of this population. Birth records and collateral records (marriage, death of relatives, birth of children) were carefully examined; these provided estimates of age that closely correlated with each other for those individuals for whom both types of records were available. These correlations strongly suggested that estimates of actual age from collateral records would be accurate if birth records were not available. Unfortunately, as seems inevitable in a detective effort of this scope, the church birth records for the community had been largely destroyed in a fire, although a few had been copied previously by the priest.

The results of Mazess and Forman's study are presented in Figure 2-1. They are striking. Up to age 70, there is a close correlation between stated age and actual age. After that age, there is a remarkable and dramatic exaggeration of age. None of the 23 individuals claiming to be over 100 was actually that old. Nor were any of the 15 persons claiming to be between 90 and 100 actually over 90. No super-centenarian has been found. Indeed, no centenarian has been found.

Why does age exaggeration occur? In each society where it occurs, prestige and authority are associated with extreme age; there are no financial or direct social benefits. Some researchers have noted a decrease in claimed birthdates when the same individual was questioned at successive times, suggesting that the repeated questioning may itself reduce the original claims.

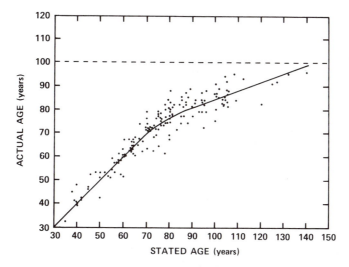

FIGURE 2-1.
The relationship between stated age and actual age in Vilcabamba, Ecuador. (Redrawn with permission from Mazess and Forman, *Journal of Gerontology* 1979, 34:94–98.)

Analysis of the USSR Shangri-La is less systematic and more anecdotal, but it gives some additional insights. Zhores Medvedev, a distinguished Russian gerontologist now living in London, has noted the important political and social motives for age exaggeration in Russia and has pointed out some unnoticed facts. For example, the famous super-centenarian Vakutia, who was reputed to be 130 years old in 1959, in reality deserted from the army during World War I and assumed his father's name through forged documents. He was only 78 years old at that time.

Among the factors Medvedev notes are many that generally concern the problem of establishing longevity:

1. As data get better, the number of centenarians decreases. In the USSR, the decrease has been about twofold over 50 years; it must be remembered that Czarist Russia was an extremely primitive society.
2. Internal passports in the USSR cannot be considered valid, since the practice dates only to 1932 and depends on oral representations of age.
3. Where most centenarians in the USSR are located, there is no birth registration at all, and 90% of the churches were destroyed between 1922 and 1940.
4. Not one of 500 famous long-lived persons claiming to be between 120 and 170 years of age could produce any reliable document of birth, marriage, education, or military service.
5. Christian populations have fewer centenarians than Moslem populations, lending credence to the thought that the Moslem ten-month year may have caused some misunderstanding.
6. Altay super-centenarians are of Mongolian and East European origin and have no birth records, yet they claim to live longer than persons of Russian origin living there since the seventeeth century, who have higher living standards and a longer average life span.
7. The survival curve of centenarians in these societies is theoretically not possible; there is no dropoff in the number of individuals at successive ages.
8. Almost all USSR inhabitants claiming ages greater than 150 have been men, and this contradicts almost all data on survival at younger ages, where women predominate.
9. The number of reported survivals of couples (both husband and wife) defies statistical averages and suggests that both ages were exaggerated.

10. Documented age exaggeration is not minor but sometimes is "two or three times."
11. The distribution of centenarians is not random; usually there is exactly one to a village, suggesting both prestige and need for an exalted elder statesman.
12. There are no intellectual or church figures with records of public activity among persons older than 108 years.
13. Physical and biochemical studies reveal a paradox. The metabolism of these claimed centenarians is that of individuals 60% of their age; in developed countries, studies of centenarians with accurately determined ages do not show such a result.

It is always possible that the next hidden and exotic society to be investigated will actually have found the secret of long life. But so far, all scientific investigations of claims of great age have failed to confirm the existence of a Shangri-La.

THE MYTH OF METHUSELAH

Perhaps there are not any extremely long-lived people in our own society, and perhaps the documentation of claims for far-off societies is a bit scanty. But there might have been people who lived for centuries and centuries in the past. Perhaps today people don't live as long as they used to. In the past, perhaps some people were nearly as old as Methuselah. The most extravagant claims of great age are biblical and are said to have occurred long ago. This theme is echoed in more recent literature, as in George Bernard Shaw's play "Back to Methuselah."

In the Book of Genesis, Adam and six of his direct descendants are reputed to have lived for over 900 years. The oldest of these patriarchs was Methuselah, at 969 years, followed by Jared (962 years), Noah (950 years), and Adam himself (930 years). Similar claims can be found in the ancient writings of other societies.

It is perhaps not worthwhile to dwell overlong on the lack of corroborating evidence for these assertions. The primary documents themselves are a matter of faith, with some faithful holding literally to the statements and others believing that the claims are allegorical. There are no supporting documents. We might conclude that, if these events did occur, they were miraculous, and we have no reason to believe that such miracles have been extended to our time.

THE MYTH OF THE FOUNTAIN

The Fountain of Youth legend can be traced back to at least 700 BC in the fable of Cyavana, an elderly Hindu priest who revealed certain religious secrets to two demigods in exchange for rejuvenation in the Pool of Youth. The Fountain theme was further elaborated in ancient Hebrew, Greek, and Roman writings. By the time Juan Ponce de León accidently discovered Florida in 1513 during his quest for the legendary Fountain of Youth, the theme was firmly established in European thought. The theme has persisted to present times, providing markets for megavitamins, mineral supplements, and even plastic surgery.

For hundreds of years, alchemists attempted to prepare rejuvenating elixirs, without success. Literally hundreds of substances, including herbs, drugs, vitamins, extracts of animal cells, fermented milk, and various serums and potions have been reported to have rejuvenating properties, without convincing evidence. In our own country, the traditional snake oil potions have fallen into disrepute, but we do still have our vitamins. Recently, the drug gerovital has been promoted by Aslan in Rumania as an agent to prevent aging. Gerovital, whose main ingredient is the local anesthetic Novocaine, has been used in treatment of Khrushchev, Sukarno, Ho Chi Minh, and other dignitaries. There exists, of course, no evidence that this agent has any such effects, and there are no a priori reasons to assume that it should. The persons cited as examples of prominent users by gerovital proponents all died, and at unremarkable ages.

In 1974, Packer and Smith published a paper in a prestigious American scientific journal reporting experiments that seemed to show that vitamin E markedly prolonged the life span of normal human fibroblast cells cultured in a laboratory flask. Later, they retracted this claim, when neither they nor others were able to reproduce the experimental results. To date, no diets, lifestyles, vitamins, drugs, or tonics have been shown to extend the human life span. Of the 4 billion human beings who have lived and died, nearly every possible combination of diet, chemical exposure, and psychological life must have existed. The absence of super-centenarians argues strongly that there is no easy track to long life, or someone would have found it by now.

The Fountain theme, however, is critical to understanding another important theme of aging. Throughout history, the idea of an extremely long life without the preservation of youth has been abhorred. The fear of being infirm in the twilight period of life recurs in the legends and literature of many cultures, past and present. Perhaps the most dramatic story is the Greek legend of Eos and Tithonus. The goddess Eos requested that Zeus give her mortal lover Tithonus eternal life. The request was granted, and Tithonus lived on forever. But he became more and more decrepit, in a classic tragedy, because Eos had failed to request eternal youth as well as eternal life. Eventually, Eos had to shut Tithonus away in a room, where he still lies, babbling constantly and unable to move. Examples of the Tithonus theme in modern literature appear in Aldous Huxley's *After Many a Summer Dies the Swan* and Oscar Wilde's *The Picture of Dorian Gray*.

RESEARCH EFFORTS IN LONGEVITY

The science of gerontology is in its infancy, and until recently there has been very little fundamental research into aging and longevity. The greatest interest has been accorded the experiments of McCay and coworkers beginning in the 1930s; they demonstrated a prolongation of the life span of laboratory rats by limitation of their food intake in early life (Figure 2-2). These experiments have been confirmed by others and are not related to specific components of diet or to weight (obesity) in adult life. In these studies, all animals were fed, beginning shortly after weaning, the same basic calorie-deficient diet with ample protein, vitamins, and minerals. Other rats were fed additional calories in the form of starch, sugar, and lard. Both the mean and the maximum life spans of the calorie-restricted rats were prolonged as compared with the other rats. On the restricted diet, the life span of male and female rats tended to equalize. The rats on restricted diets were said to retain a youthful appearance (for a rat) and had a delay in onset of chronic diseases. They also grew to smaller adult sizes and were more susceptible to accidental death in early life.

Ross (1961) extended these initial observations in a more detailed set of experiments employing precise regulation of protein, fat, carbohydrates, minerals, vitamins, and trace elements in the diets of male laboratory rats. Ross' data confirmed McCay's observations and also showed that, in addition to total caloric restriction, the ratio of protein to carbohydrates could influence rat life expectancy (Figure 2-3).

The meaning of these results is uncertain if one attempts to apply them to human life spans. The maximum rat life span is not known, since laboratory rats

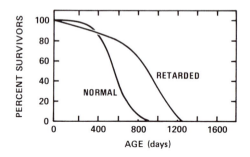
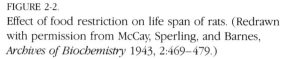

FIGURE 2-2.
Effect of food restriction on life span of rats. (Redrawn
with permission from McCay, Sperling, and Barnes,
Archives of Biochemistry 1943, 2:469–479.)

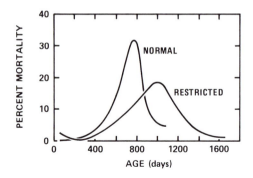
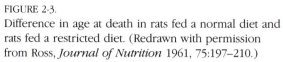

FIGURE 2-3.
Difference in age at death in rats fed a normal diet and
rats fed a restricted diet. (Redrawn with permission
from Ross, *Journal of Nutrition* 1961, 75:197–210.)

live in a stimulus-deprived environment and optimal nutritional and environmental conditions have not been established. The rat survival curves did not
approach the degree of rectangularization seen in human curves for the developed nations, even though rats dying early in life were excluded from the analyses in many of the experiments. Human beings in 1980 in the United States live
an average of about 70 years with a standard deviation of 5 years, or about one-

fourteenth of the average life expectancy. Ross' laboratory rats lived 632 days with a standard deviation of 125 days, or about one-fifth of their average life expectancy. It seems to us that these investigators have succeeded in increasing the rats' life expectancy but *not* their life span. Certainly, humans who are calorie deprived in childhood do not live exceptionally long. It seems likely that the maximal rat life span is yet longer than 632 days and that these experiments merely prolonged life expectancy from quite subnatural length to somewhat less subnatural length.

Other scientific approaches to the study of longevity have focused on observations of phenomena of premature aging. Several human syndromes demonstrate characteristics of early "aging." Although very few patients exhibit these syndromes, they have been intensely studied. Progeria, also called the Hutchinson–Gilford syndrome, is perhaps the best example.

Patients with progeria appear normal at birth. Within the first two years of life, they develop profound growth retardation. They develop a characteristic "plucked bird" appearance, with loss of scalp hair and subcutaneous fat, prominent scalp veins, protruding ears with absent lobes, a thin, beaked nose, and a small jaw contrasted with a normal-sized cranial vault. Their skin appears aged, with irregular spotty pigmentation. Mental and motor functions are normal. These patients develop severe atherosclerosis at an early age and usually die from heart disease in their second decade; the mean age at death is about 13 years. Obviously, progeria is a caricature of aging; many abnormalities are present that are not found in normal elderly people, and many disorders of elderly people (such as arthritis, cataracts, senility, decreased hearing, and malignant tumors) are not found in patients with progeria.

Werner's syndrome is another caricature of aging. These patients develop the syndrome between 10 and 40 years of age. The earliest sign is graying of the hair, followed by atrophy of the skin, with eventual ulceration, loss of hair, high-pitched or hoarse voice, and diabetes. Patients with Werner's syndrome have short stature, profound muscle wasting, senile appearance, osteoporosis, atherosclerosis, and malignant tumors (usually sarcomas). Death occurs at a mean age of 47 years and results most often from atherosclerosis or malignancy. The cause of this genetic disorder is unknown.

There are other disorders, such as Rothmund's syndrome and Cockayne's syndrome, that are caricatures of aging. None exactly mimics natural aging, and few insights have emerged from study of these unfortunate individuals.

THE TAIL OF THE CURVE

Perhaps the observations that best demonstrate the biological limit to the life span come from the current data on long life, summarized for the United States in Table 2-1. If superlongevity were soon to be possible, there should be some exceptional individuals who would anticipate the future, who would break the statistical distributions that indicate a barrier to immortality.

But the tail of the human survival curve is smooth and follows normal biological (Gaussian) distribution principles. Of those reaching the age of 85, only one in 10,000 will reach the age of 110. At each interval, the expected dropoff occurs. The curve has the force of biological law, and there are no exceptions.

TABLE 2-1.
Number of Deaths at Selected Specific Ages, United States, 1975

Age	Number of deaths
85 years	42,320
90 years	24,115
95 years	7,842
100 years	1,392
105 years	186
110 years	24
Total deaths 85 years and older	280,077

Source: *Vital Statistics of the United States, 1975.* U.S. Public Health Service, Bureau of Health Statistics, Washington, D.C.

A SYNTHESIS

A survey of both myth and medicine indicates that the quest for immortality is and always has been a futile one. Equally important, it suggests that the search is misplaced and that the quest for preservation of youthful vigor provides the underlying force. The data suggest that lifestyles of activity and moderation are associated with relative longevity in some cultures. They suggest that, even in the absence of disease, a natural life span and a natural death are intrinsic to our biology.

These observations emphasize the need to focus on disorders that prematurely affect the elderly and cut short their years of natural life. Lewis Thomas, in a marvelous essay entitled "Medical Lessons from History," gives direction to the new quest. "In short," Thomas writes, "I believe that the major diseases of human beings have become approachable biological puzzles, ultimately solvable. It follows from this that it is now possible to begin thinking about a human society relatively free of disease. This would surely have been an unthinkable notion a half century ago, and oddly enough it has a rather apocalyptic sound today. What will we do about dying, and about all that population, if such things were to come about? What can we die of, if not disease?"

The answer, to be developed in coming chapters, is that we will die a natural death, just modestly prolonged from our present life expectancy, but without an extended period of infirmity. We will not find the solution for the riddle of Methuselah, but there is a sense in which we may be able to locate the Fountain.

Little of all we value here
Wakes on the morn of its hundredth year
Without both feeling and looking queer.
In fact, there's nothing that keeps its youth,
So far as I know, but a tree and truth.

CHAPTER THREE

AGING AND THE RECTANGULAR CURVE

wherein the survival curves of people and animals
begin to assume a curious shape

A finite life span has been confirmed for
many species and for many eras. There is a characteristic maximum life span for
each species—3 years for rats, about 40 years for horses, about 50 years for apes,
and over 100 years for humans. The finite maximum life span must stand as one
of the central facts of the study of aging.

Sacher and others, using anthropological data, have worked to link maximum
life span to other biological features for a variety of mammals. They have studied
85 mammalian species, ranging in size from shrews to elephants. There are
strong correlations between brain size/body weight ratio and maximum species
life span. Cutler has used such analyses to calculate, elegantly, the maximum life
span of *Homo sapiens* and related ancestors, as shown in Table 3-1. The fascinating finding from these calculations is that the maximum human life span
shows a steady increase, resulting in a doubling, over a period of some 3 million
years ending 100,000 years ago. Since that time, anthropological estimates indicate that there has been no change. As we mentioned in the previous chapter

TABLE 3-1.
Maximum Life Span in Primates

Genus and species	Common name	Life Span		Time of appearance (years ago)
		Observed	Predicted	
Presbytis entellus	Langur	22	24	
Macaca mulatta	Rhesus monkey	29	27	
Papio cynocephalus	Western baboon	32	35	
Hylobates lar	Gibbon	32	30	
Pongo pygmaeus	Orangutan	50	41	
Gorilla gorilla	Gorilla	40	42	
Pan troglodytes	Chimpanzee	45	46	
Homo sapiens	Man	95	92	
Ramapithecus	Hominid	—	42	14,000,000
Australopithecus	Hominid	35	51	3,000,000
Homo habilis		—	61	1,500,000
Homo erectus		50	69	700,000
Homo europeaus		50	89	100,000
Homo neanderthalensis		50	93	45,000
Homo sapiens europeaeus		—	94	15,000
Homo sapiens recens		90	94	10,000
Homo sapiens modern		95	92	present

Source: After Cutler, "Evolution of Human Longevity and the Genetic Complexity Governing Aging Rate." *Proceedings of the National Academy of Sciences* 1975, 72:4664–4668.

and will discuss in greater detail later, there is good contemporary evidence for lack of change in the maximum life span during the last century. The record of nature suggests a much stronger conclusion; there has been no change in the past 1000 centuries.

Certainly, such estimations are fraught with difficulty, and they are based on incomplete data. Yet they strongly support the concept of species-specific finite life spans. In this chapter, we will begin to develop the reasoning that has led to the concepts of a fixed life span and natural death. We begin with the important concept of the rectangular curve.

GOMPERTZ'S LAW

We are not sure of the origin of the term *rectangular* as applied to the survival curves of humans or other species, but it appears in the writings of gerontologists and actuaries in the United States as early as 1922. The concept almost certainly has its intellectual roots in a paper published by Benjamin Gompertz in 1825, "On the Nature of the Function Expressive of the Law of Human Mortality."

Gompertz studied human vital statistics from four locations, Northampton, Deparcieux, Sweden, and Carlisle. He observed that an exponential increase in death rate occurred between the ages of 10 and 60. Plotted on a logarithmic scale, the age-specific death rate showed an increase that was nearly linear. Gompertz, and later, Makeham (see Greenwood, 1928, and Henderson, 1915), suggested that human mortality was governed by an equation with two terms, the first accounting for chance deaths that could occur at any age, and the second representing the exponential increase with time, seen to be a characteristic of the species. On these perceptive observations has been built much of the theory of human aging. Gompertz's law can now be seen to be slightly less than a natural law, but it serves as a reasonably accurate description of human mortality in many societies.

Most readers will not be interested in the intricacies of the various statistical calculations, and we have removed them to the appendices. It is important, however, to have a general concept of the way in which survival data are presented. There are three basic graphic representations, and they are shown in Figures 3-1, 3-2, and 3-3. Each of them portrays a different aspect of the same survival data for the United States in 1910 and 1970.

First, the number of deaths occurring at each age can be plotted on a graph. Such a graph, as in Figure 3-1, shows clearly the magnitude of infant mortality, the early life period with few deaths, and the increasing number of deaths thereafter, until finally, with few survivors, the total number of deaths decreases again. Total deaths (D_x) at each age (x) are one column of a standard life table. Note that the curves are not smooth over the ages of 15 to 25; this irregularity represents traumatic deaths, which peak during these ages.

Second, the death rate, rather than the total number of deaths, can be plotted against year of age (Figure 3-2). The age-specific death rate (R_x) takes into account a "denominator," which is the number of persons alive at that age and is usually expressed as deaths per 1000 individuals per year. Figure 3-2 also shows the infant mortality, the early life period with few deaths, and the later rise in mortality rate, but here the curve continues upward since the death rate continues to accelerate with advancing age until the end of the life span. Because the death rate (R_x) increases so markedly, it is convenient to plot such curves on a logarithmic scale for better visibility. Gompertz's law was formulated from such a plot. After the age of 30, a nearly linear rise can be seen, with the death rate doubling about every eight years. Again, note the marked "trauma bump" at age

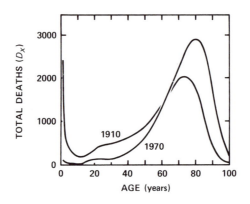

FIGURE 3-1.
Total deaths per year are plotted at each age for the United States in the years 1910
and 1970. There is a decrease in early deaths with a corresponding increase in late
deaths in 1970 as compared with 1910. (Data for 1910 are from the United States vital
statistics in L. I. Dublin, "The Possibility of Extending Human Life," in *The Harvey
Lectures, 1922–1923.* Data for 1970 are from *Vital Statistics of the United States,*
National Center for Health Statistics, 1970.)

20. In 1970, the relative importance of trauma had increased greatly; such deaths
made up nearly 75% of all deaths between ages 15 and 25. We suspect that the
Gompertz plot essentially consists of two straight lines, one declining exponentially from birth and representing inescapable deaths very early in life in non-
viable individuals, and the second rising exponentially from birth.

Third, the number of persons living (L_x) at the beginning of a particular age
(x) can be calculated, starting with an initial population of, say, 100,000. This
curve represents the final column in most life tables and produces the most
familiar survival curve. It is the easiest curve to visualize. Figure 3-3 shows these
survival curves for 1910 and 1970. The two curves show the same maximum life
span of about 100 years, with an upward projection to the right for 1970 as early
deaths declined. This phenomenon is termed *rectangularization of the survival
curve.*

The mortality rate (R_x) is plotted for five different societies in Figure 3-4. One
of the most remarkable features of these curves, as in Figure 3-2, is that, following
an early elevated mortality rate, there occurs a minimum at about 11 years of
age. This same phenomenon occurs for many other societies not depicted in
Figure 3-4. Thus it appears that, in all societies, independent of environmental
conditions, the probability of death is lowest just before puberty at about 11

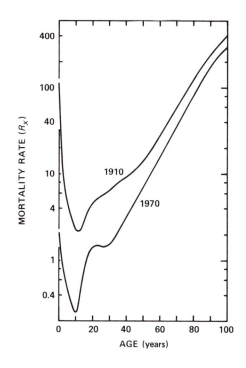

FIGURE 3-2.
The age-specific mortality rate (number of deaths per year per 1000 individuals entering each age) is shown at each age for the United States in the years 1910 and 1970. For both years, the mortality rate is minimal at about age 11 and shows a steady exponential increase following the age of 30. (Data from the same sources cited for Figure 3-1.)

years of age. After the age of 11, there occurs in all societies an upward sloping of the mortality rate, eventually reaching a steady slope sometime after 30 years of age; in this final phase, the mortality rate doubles about every eight years. In all societies, the mortality rates at very old ages are about the same. The important observation here, as Gompertz noted, is that the mortality rate displays an exponential increase at some point after the age of 30. An exponential increase in mortality rate mandates a finite species life span.

Figures 3-1, 3-2, and 3-3 plot data from the United States in 1910 and 1970. In Figure 3-1, deaths are seen to occur at a later age in 1970; thus the curve for 1970 has a higher peak. In Figure 3-2, the starting point for the steep exponential portion of the curve can be seen to have moved from about age 45 in 1910 to

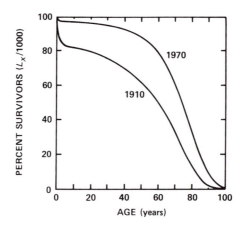

FIGURE 3-3.
These survival curves for the United States in 1910 and 1970 are calculated from the mortality rates shown in Figure 3-2, starting with 100,000 live births (L_0). The curves show a rectangularization effect between 1910 and 1970 with increased survival to older ages and a fixed maximum life span. (Data from the same sources cited for Figure 3-1.)

about age 30 in 1970, with the same doubling period of about eight years. In Figure 3-3, we see that the curve has become more rectangular for 1970 than it was for 1910.

THE RECTANGULAR CURVE

Survival curves for animals show a similar pattern of rectangularization with domestication or better care. Old age in wild animals is very rare, as it probably was for prehistoric man living in a dangerous environment. In uncivilized environments, accidental deaths and violent deaths account for a greater proportion of deaths than the biologically determined life-span limit. For the great majority of wild animal species, there is a very high neonatal mortality, followed by an adult mortality rate that is almost as high and is nearly independent of age. In such environments, death occurs mostly as a result of accidents and attacks by predators. One day is about as dangerous as the next.

By contrast, animals in captivity begin to show survival curves much more rectangular in shape. Such animals are removed from most threats by accident

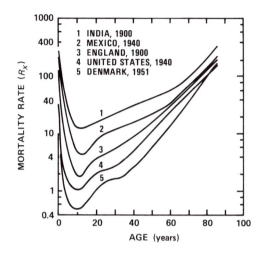

FIGURE 3-4.
The age-specific mortality rate in different countries.
(Redrawn with permission from Jones, "A Special
Consideration of the Aging Process, Disease, and Life
Expectancy." *Advances in Biological and Medical
Physics* 1956, 4:281–337.)

or predator, and for them the second term of the equation, that of the species
life span, begins to dominate. Figure 3-5 shows theoretical calculations of this
phenomenon after Sacher (1977). Such rectangularization has been documented
for many animals, including dogs, horses, birds, voles, rats, and flies.

DECLINE IN ORGAN FUNCTION WITH AGE

Gompertz's studies of human populations strongly indicate that it is possible to
die of old age, independent of specific accident or major illness. In other words,
even if the Makeham term representing chance deaths is reduced to zero, the
Gompertz term with exponential increase in age-specific death rate mandates a
fixed natural life expectancy for a species. The data in Table 2-1 show this result.
But how can death without disease occur? What can be the cause of death? Why
will the organism cease to function? Most students of the aging process find
these questions answered in careful studies of organ reserve, as developed and
presented most cogently by Nathan Shock (1977).

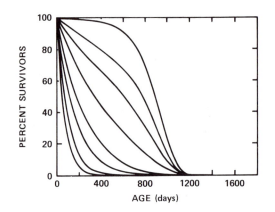

FIGURE 3-5.
Theoretical survival curves for an animal become progressively more rectangular as the environment progresses from wild to domestic. (Redrawn with permission from Sacher, "Life Table Modification and Life Prolongation," in L. Hayflick and C. E. Finch, eds., *Handbook of the Biology of Aging,* Van Nostrand Reinhold, 1977.)

Figure 3-6 is drawn from the data Shock developed in 1960, and it is modified only slightly from what has been called "the most frequently shown data in the field of gerontology." The data show that many important physiological functions decline with age, and the decline is quite close to being a straight line. It is important to emphasize that these data were obtained from healthy human subjects in whom no disease could be identified that was related to the function being measured. Thus, the observed decline does not depend on disease.

Figure 3-6 is a major oversimplification of complex data, and some of the idiosyncrasies in these data will be discussed in later chapters. The lines are not actually as straight as portrayed, and some of the data have been contested. The point is that a considerable body of research supports a gradual, nearly linear decrease in organ function with age.

Normal, healthy organisms maintain an excess organ reserve beyond immediate functional needs. We have four to ten times as much reserve function as we need in the resting state. The heart during exercise can increase its output sixfold or more. The kidneys can still excrete waste products adequately if five-sixths of the functional units, the nephrons, are destroyed. Surgeons can remove one entire lung, and sometimes part of the second, and still have an operative success. Three-fourths of the liver can be removed, under some circumstances, and life is still maintained.

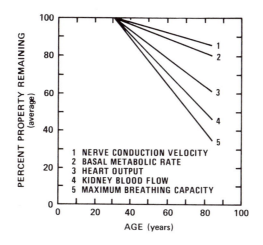

FIGURE 3-6.
The linear decline of organ function with increasing age. (Redrawn with permission from Shock, "Discussion on Mortality and Measurement of Aging," in B. L. Strehler, S. D. Ebert, H. B. Glass, and N. W. Shock, eds., *The Biology of Aging: A Symposium,* © 1960, American Institute of Biological Sciences.)

However, the mean level of reserve in many of our organs declines as we grow older. We seldom notice this gradual loss of our organ reserve. Only in the circumstances of exceptional stress do we need all that excess function anyway. Shock and others suggest that the decline may be plotted as a straight line.

HOMEOSTASIS AND ORGAN RESERVE

The human body may be viewed as a remarkable assembly of components functioning at various levels of organization. Systems of molecules, cells, and organs are all marvelously integrated to preserve life. The eminent nineteenth-century physiologist Claude Bernard emphasized that these integrated components act to maintain a constant internal environment despite variable external conditions. Bernard saw life as a conflict between external threats and the ability of the organism to maintain the internal milieu.

These fundamental observations have stood well the test of time. Indeed, the human organism cannot survive if the body temperature is more than a few degrees from normal, if acid–base balance is disturbed by a single *p*H unit, or if more than 20% of the body water is lost. Body chemicals are regulated closely, often to within 2% or 3% of an average value. A change in one direction in a body constituent is often followed by a complicated set of responses that act to restore equilibrium.

Bernard also noted that living beings change from a period of development to a period of senescence or decline. He stated that "this characteristic of a determined development, of a beginning and an end, of continuous progress in one direction within a fixed term, belongs inherently to living beings."

The regulation of bodily functions within precise limits was termed *homeostasis* by Cannon (1932). Living organisms under threat from an extraordinary array of destructive sources maintain their internal milieu despite the perturbations, using what Cannon called the "wisdom of the body." Dubos (1965) has pointed out that this "wisdom" is not infallible. Homeostasis is only an ideal concept; regulatory mechanisms do not always return bodily functions to their original state, and they can sometimes be misdirected. Dubos sees disease as a "manifestation of such inadequate responses." Health corresponds to the situation in which the organism responds adaptively and restores its original integrity.

The ability of the body to maintain homeostasis declines inevitably with decreasing organ reserve. Figure 3-6 shows the decline for lungs, kidneys, heart, and nerves. The decline is not the same for all individuals, nor is the decline the same for all organs. For example, nerve conduction declines more slowly than does maximal breathing capacity. And some organs, such as the liver, intestinal lining cells, and bone marrow red cells, seem to show even less decline with age.

The important point, however, is that with age there is a decline in the ability to respond to perturbations. With the decline in organ reserve, the protective envelope within which a disturbance may be restored becomes smaller. A young person might survive a major injury or a bacterial pneumonia; an older person may succumb to a fractured hip or to influenza. If homeostasis cannot be maintained, life is over. The declining straight lines of Figure 3-6 clearly mandate a finite life span; death must inevitably result when organ function declines below the level necessary to sustain life.

A GENERAL THEORY OF MORTALITY

Careful analysis of the mortality data and physiological functions enabled Strehler and Mildvan (1960) to develop a mathematical model representing a general theory of mortality and aging. The model very closely fits observed data for different species and different human cultures.

This elegant theory begins with the two basic principles we have just discussed, Gompertz's exponential increase in mortality rate with age and the linear decline in physiological functions illustrated by the data of Shock and others. By casting the question in the context of the statistics used in the kinetic theory equations of classical physics, Strehler and Mildvan were able to resolve the apparent contradiction between a linear decline in vitality and an exponential increase in death rates.

Strehler and Mildvan see the organism as composed of a number of independent physiological subsystems that are continually subject to displacement by fluctuations in the internal or external environment. Energy is required for the organism to overcome the displacement and to restore homeostasis. The maximum rate at which the organism can expend such energy is a measure of the organism's vitality. Death results when an environmental challenge is greater than the vitality of the organism. Environmental challenges, considered to be approximately random, have varying magnitudes. If the magnitudes of these challenges display an exponential frequency distribution (that is, large challenges being less frequent than small ones), then, when vitality decreases linearly, the mortality rate will increase exponentially. Appendix C summarizes the mathematical expressions that describe these relationships.

Strehler and Mildvan use an interesting transformation to plot the data of Figure 3-6 in terms of percent reserve capacity. Such a representation makes the decline not only linear but similar in slope for different organs. At age 85, less than 50% of the original reserve capacity remains, as is shown in Figure 3-7.

These mathematical representations fit known data extraordinarily well, and they allow estimation of mortality effects of environmental challenges, such as radiation exposure, to be calculated quite accurately. The theory predicts a maximum human life span of 103 years, a linear loss of physiological function with age of 0.9% to 1.4% of the maximal reserve per year, and a ratio of maximum reserve capacity to average demand of between 7 and 11. Independent data are in reasonable agreement with these values.

Figure 3-8 shows this relationship schematically. A linear decline in two organ systems is shown. The central core represents the normal narrow limits of homeostasis, and the outer envelope represents the most severe disturbance the organism can restore by using all remaining reserve capacity. The vital areas represented in cross-section will shrink by a factor of four when the reserve of each organ has decreased linearly by a factor of two. The actual situation, of course, has many more dimensions. A given random challenge may come from

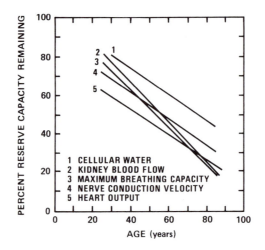

FIGURE 3-7.
The linear decline of organ reserve with increasing age.
(Redrawn with permission from Strehler and Mildvan,
"General Theory of Mortality and Aging," *Science* 1960,
132:14–21. Copyright 1960 by the American Association
for the Advancement of Science.)

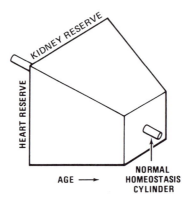

FIGURE 3-8.
Diminishing area of homeostasis with the decline in heart and kidney reserve. Linear
decline in organ reserve in the several organs results in an exponential decline in the
area representing vitality of the entire organism. A challenge to the organism that
carries outside the outer homeostatic envelope will result in death.

any direction and may stress one or more reserve capacities. If organ reserve is relatively preserved in some organs, survival is enhanced, since the likelihood of challenge from a vulnerable direction is decreased. This intuitive representation approximates the complex mathematical model; a linear decline in organ reserve in multiple organs results in an exponential increase in mortality rate.

Can we find medical examples of these phenomena? Indeed, yes. Pneumonia as "the old man's friend" is one such example. An aged person without organ reserve may die swiftly and easily during the early stages of a pulmonary infection that would not have troubled a young person with ample reserve vitality. The marked increase in national death rates during influenza epidemics is a second example. The likelihood of death from this moderately benign infection is very small in young adults but rises steeply in the aged and in others without sufficient organ reserve. The national recommendations for persons who should receive influenza vaccines reflect these observations. A third example is the well-known observation that medication doses must be sharply reduced in older individuals without organ reserve; this observation is a medical first principle for good physicians caring for the elderly. Since drugs tend to override homeostatic mechanisms, normal drug doses can easily result in "overshoot." If the patient has no reserve homeostasis to correct the new threat, and if the overshoot has extended beyond the vital envelope, death may result.

Precisely because they seem at first to be totally unrelated, the data of Figure 3-9 serve to underscore these points. Here, the presence of organ reserve is shown to be necessary for successful function as a pedestrian. Despite lesser activity and greater caution by the elderly, decreased reserve function means less success at avoiding the environmental challenge posed by passing automobiles. Hearing, eyesight, reflexes, cardiopulmonary reserve, and muscular reserve are all decreased, and these factors combine to make avoidable causes of death less avoidable.

EVOLUTION AND AGING

The reasons for the finite life span are not simple. As an introduction to the relationship between genetic evolution and aging, first consider a common example. If you are responsible for making automobiles, you do not plan for the automobiles you make to break down, and you do not plant time bombs in them to ensure the finitude of their life span. Rather, you build them just well enough

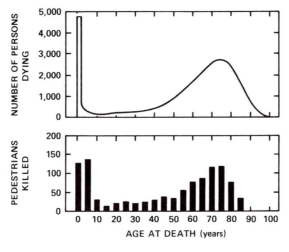

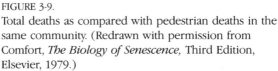

FIGURE 3-9.
Total deaths as compared with pedestrian deaths in the
same community. (Redrawn with permission from
Comfort, *The Biology of Senescence,* Third Edition,
Elsevier, 1979.)

to last as long as they have to. First, almost all cars should function well through
the warranty period before the first system breakdown occurs—otherwise, your
company's expenses will increase. Second, the car should remain in satisfactory
condition until the first owner is ready to sell it, perhaps two to six years. If the
car does not last this long, the owner is not likely to purchase another of your
automobiles.

Since you do not know the conditions under which each car will be used, and
since the cars are not exactly the same in quality due to inevitable problems in
your manufacturing plant, you throw in a reserve factor. Perhaps you say to your
foremen, "Build them so that they last eight years or 80,000 miles." Still, you are
soon under attack for building automobiles that "self-destruct." Such phrases as
"self-destruct" and "planned obsolescence" contain irony and satire but are not
strictly accurate. You didn't build the automobiles to self-destruct. You just didn't
build them to last very long.

This mundane scenario displays exactly the confusion between plan and effect
that has plagued understanding of evolution and aging. Recently, speculation has

been raised about genes that might be responsible for aging. The reasoning has gone something like this: "Since longevity clearly runs in families, it must be under genetic control. There must be genes, then, that cause us to self-destruct." Of course, no evidence for such genes has ever been found, and the whole theory is a bit ludicrous when you think about it. "Wearing out" does not seem likely to be under positive genetic control. There doesn't seem to be much reason for a genetic time bomb.

Since Darwin, evolutionary theory holds that the fittest offspring reproduce and the less fit do not, so that gradually a species comes to be made up of its fittest members. But after the reproductive years, the fitness of the organism does not directly contribute to the fitness of the offspring; the genetic material has already been passed.

So, after the age of about 35, when reproduction is completed, there is no further direct evolutionary advantage to longevity. But there remain indirect selective advantages. Progeny with living parents are more likely to be protected until they also reach reproductive ages, and, in human beings, development continues for some eighteen years. So, natural selection could possibly operate until the age of 50, or 55, or even somewhat higher, if one grants a (much weaker) selective advantage to having grandparents to pass down the tribal wisdom and to serve as surrogate parents in case of accident to the actual parents. Beyond this, the argument gets truly tenuous.

For species survival, granted hardship and variability, reserve needs to be built into the individual. Thus, given the human age of puberty, one might speculate that most individuals should live 70 years or so without serious malfunction. As in our automobile analogy, the body seems to be designed to outlast the warranty period (puberty) and the period of initial ownership (parenthood), with enough reserve to ensure that most individuals will survive these stages without a serious breakdown. After that, both you and your automobile are on linear lines of decay of performance of components, and on exponential lines of likelihood of total breakdown.

Sacher (1978) has eloquently argued these points and has demonstrated that they hold statistically across species and across eras. He notes that "organisms are inherently fallible and finite in their life processes and that the aging and failure they experience are due either to intrinsic limitations of their own functioning or to spontaneous molecular degradations inherent in the finite rate of entropy production in metabolizing systems. The radical implication of this process is that aging does not exist as an ontological reality." Each species has evolved with its own aging process limits, not from the control of "aging genes" but rather as the totality of rates of failure inherent in the imperfect execution of its genetically determined "proper" functions.

There are not many who will still argue for the elusive senescence genes, postulated to have benign expression in early life and then to switch to a deleterious "senescent" expression after the end of reproductive life. The search was futile. Probably, aging just happens, as the result of cumulative, random, and inevitable errors in translation of DNA into protein. The errors may even be a crucial part of a process that allows variation among individuals and thus allows natural selection. Errors in the transcription of parent DNA into daughter DNA are clearly necessary to produce the genetic changes that underlie natural selection. Similarly, molecular errors in the transcription of DNA into RNA or the translation of RNA into protein may underlie aging.

Now in building of chaises, I tell you what,
There is always *somewhere* a weakest spot,—
In hub, tire, felloe, in spring or thill,
In panel, or crossbar, or floor, or sill,
In screw, bolt, thoroughbrace,—lurking still,
Find it somewhere you must and will,—

CHAPTER FOUR

THE HAYFLICK LIMIT

*wherein cells and tissues appear to have
discrete and finite life spans*

The philosopher's stone and the search for the Fountain of Youth epitomize a basic human yearning for control of life, aging, and death. Reasoning about these processes, until this century, was of necessity theoretical, somewhat superficial, inherently unprovable, and in the last analysis rather unsatisfactory. Even recently, scientific approaches to more precisely formulated questions have focused on disease rather than its absence and on curative therapy rather than on understanding the basic nature of life processes. Today, the increasing number of senior citizens, their increasing consumption of the national health dollar, and the new set of illnesses they are subject to has resulted in two new specialties—gerontology (the study of aging) and geriatrics (the care of elderly patients). The laboratory scientist has begun to look seriously at some traditional philosophical questions but, in a curious choice of terms, speaks of the negative aging rather than the positive immortality and of the negative senescence rather than the preservation of youth.

The addressable questions cut right to the heart of the matter. What is the barrier to immortality? Why is the life span fixed? Why do we age? Can the process of aging be altered? How? What are the consequences of such alteration?

In the past, some scientists have reasoned that, if the species life span is fixed, this must be a genetic phenomenon, so we may search for genes that control aging. Is the genetic control fixed at the level of the individual cell, so that we are the personal owners of a large collection of aging cellular constituents? Or is control exercised through mechanisms within the cell, at an even more fundamental level, so that problems with our mitochondria, or our DNA, are responsible for our growing old? Or could aging be controlled at the level of the organ, so that our cardiac reserve, or our arterial reserve, or our kidney reserve becomes the limiting factor for life? Or is the control a central one, from the brain, perhaps the hypothalamus, whence could come influences affecting all cells and all organs?

The earliest reasoning about these questions tended to miss the point. In Chapter Three we discussed evolutionary forces and genetic controls, concluding that the absence of genetic control rather than its presence allows us to age and that natural selection cannot operate to increase the species life span. This observation is increasingly the standard theory, and it results in turning the fundamental questions around. We now look for basic mechanisms of aging, not control mechanisms, and several tantalizing explanations of why we age have been developed.

The discussion that follows is a bit technical, so we will give the conclusions in advance. There are cellular and subcellular mechanisms that result in a finite life span for some but not all cells. Criticisms of such studies are not as strong as the studies themselves. Genetic errors, which may underlie aging, must exist, or other essential characteristics of our species could not exist. The close relationship between cellular immortality and malignant change suggests that, even if an approach to modification of cellular aging could be developed, its use in human beings would not be prudent until observations of its effects in many animal species and in small numbers of people had been carried out for several centuries. So, the finite life span remains a certainty in our time.

Current theories of aging build on ancient foundations. Hippocrates postulated that the life force was innate body heat, which emanated from the heart. In his view, aging resulted from a diminution of the total reserve of this innate heat. Aristotle added the view that natural death occurred in old age because of the low reserve of innate heat, since even a slight illness or perturbation could extinguish life. Galen clearly separated the aging process from specific diseases, and he postulated that not only heat but also moisture was lost with age; he concluded, "That which all men commonly call old age is the dry and cold constitution of the body resulting from many years of life."

The discovery of the structure of DNA in the early 1950s gave new life to the study of aging and allowed new theoretical formulations to be raised. Yet, experimental confirmation of the theories has proved difficult. Most authorities now consider aging to be a complex process resulting from interplay of a number of factors, although it remains a tenable position to maintain simply that a single, simple molecular explanation of aging has not yet been discovered.

There exists a body of undisputed fact. Following puberty, inexorable changes occur in a number of bodily functions. This phenomenon, discussed in Chapter Three as decline in homeostasis, appears remarkably general and applies at least roughly to all major functions that have been studied. With loss of capacity, the organism is increasingly susceptible to disease or accident, and ultimately death must result from continuation of these decay processes. But at what level does the decay occur?

CELLULAR AGING

The most provocative and the best-established observations suggest the importance of the cellular level. It has been possible for many years to culture human or animal cells in the laboratory and to monitor closely events within these isolated cells—to study life outside a living organism. Beginning in 1912, Carrell and Ebeling conducted a series of experiments in which normal chick embryo cells (fibroblasts) were continuously cultured in the laboratory without senescent decay being apparent. It seemed that they had succeeded in demonstrating that the cell was potentially immortal.

Certain cells, such as the precursors of eggs and spermatozoa, must indeed be immortal. If they were not, the species could not survive, since this history of the species can be viewed as the successive dividing, over and over again, of the original seed. And other investigators have convincingly demonstrated that some cancer cells can divide indefinitely. Under optimum conditions, human malignant cells, such as HeLa cells derived from cervical cancer, can be propagated by culture and reculture through an immense and seemingly endless series of divisions.

The nub of the question is the somatic cells, however. There are three categories of these cells, each with different aging characteristics. First, there are continuous mitotic cells, such as intestinal lining cells, bone marrow cells, and the superficial skin cells. These continue to divide throughout our life, and wounds in them can be healed by regeneration. Their rate of division may decrease slightly with age, but they show only slight loss of functional capability during the human life span. Second, there are intermittently dividing cells, such as liver cells and fibroblasts, which normally divide very slowly. But, in response to injury, they can divide rapidly and regenerate the injured part. Finally, there are postmitotic cells, such as nerve cells and muscle cells, which do not divide at all during adult life but nevertheless appear to undergo degenerative changes with time. These cells can repair themselves after injury if the nucleus of the cell is still alive, but no new cells can be made. Are somatic cells in any or all of these categories potentially immortal?

The Carrell experiments suggested that they were, that culture of fibroblasts isolated in the laboratory could be carried out forever. These experiments had a profound influence on theories of aging. If normal somatic cells removed from an intact animal could be propagated indefinitely in the laboratory, then aging must not occur at the cellular level. Immortality is theoretically possible. We need only find the control mechanism and modify it.

Unfortunately, these data could not be confirmed in other laboratories. Inadvertently, the cultures had been contaminated with fresh chick embryo fibroblasts during culturing processes. Fibroblasts had not been shown to be immortal. Conceptually, these experiments retarded the field of aging research, since they led many investigators down the wrong path.

In 1961, Hayflick and Moorhead published a landmark paper demonstrating that normal human fibroblast cells have a strictly limited life span in tissue culture; normal embryo fibroblasts divide about 50 times and no more. This careful work has been confirmed and extended by many investigators and is central to understanding the current state of the science. It results in the concept of the Hayflick limit.

Tissue culture studies have many limitations, and these experiments almost certainly do not literally depict the actual aging process. We present the arguments here as an important analogy, indicating that some steady-state biological functions have built-in time limits and that the existence of such time limits reinforces the concept of a finite life span.

Hayflick and Moorhead isolated fibroblast cells from human fetal tissues, such as lung, skin, muscle, heart, liver, and kidney. Placed in a flask with liquid tissue culture medium, the cells were grown until they formed a layer of cells across the bottom of the flask. After formation of this primary culture, the enzyme trypsin was added to break the attachments between the cells, which were then divided in half and cultured again to confluence in two new flasks. This subcultivation produces a population doubling, since just enough cells to cover the bottom of one flask become just enough to cover the bottom of two flasks. And the process can be repeated until the cells no longer proliferate. The sequence is illustrated in Figure 4-1.

Dramatically, neither of the two results that might have been expected actually occurred. One might have thought that the cells would have proved immortal; since the environment was always the same, there would be no reason for any change to occur. Or, one might have expected that each generation would show more aging changes than the preceding generation and that eventually the subcultures would not be able to be maintained. What happened was yet more remarkable; the cells divided vigorously for many subcultivations, then gradually developed biochemical changes and ceased to divide after just a few more subcultivations. The number of doublings averaged 50 in different experiments with embryo-derived cultures, with a range from about 40 to about 60.

This pattern of "aging in the bottle" is now erroneously called *clonal senescence* (since the cultures are not clones). The barrier to indefinite replication is called the Hayflick limit. It is shown graphically in Figure 4-2. There are three distinct phases of growth. Phase I is the primary culture, where fibroblast cells initially form a confluent layer in the first flask after isolation from human tissue. This takes from one to three weeks and represents a period of cell adjustment to the culture conditions. Phase II begins with the first subcultivation of cells. There is vigorous growth with numerous population doublings occurring over many months, at intervals from 23 hours to about a week. This phase ends as the cells begin to slow their rate of division. Phase III demonstrates greatly diminished cell division, the appearance of debris within cells, and numerous other intracellular changes. Phase III is irreversible.

Detailed analysis of these experiments by many investigators leads to the conclusion that the Hayflick limit is an intrinsic characteristic of the cells. There is no evidence that cell decay results from toxic or infectious agents in the growth media. The experiments have been exhaustively confirmed, and the onset of

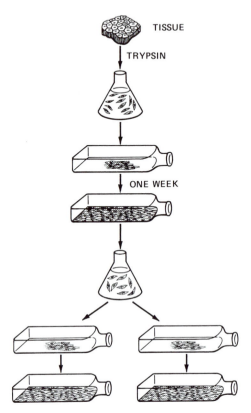

TISSUE

TRYPSIN

ONE WEEK

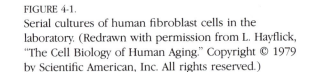

FIGURE 4-1.
Serial cultures of human fibroblast cells in the
laboratory. (Redrawn with permission from L. Hayflick,
"The Cell Biology of Human Aging." Copyright © 1979
by Scientific American, Inc. All rights reserved.)

Phase III is nearly always between 40 and 60 population doublings for embryo
cells.

In 1962, Hayflick froze many vials of embryo cells that had completed several
population doublings. Freezing simply arrests the growth, which resumes when
the cells are returned to normal temperatures. Each year since that time, some
of these vials have been thawed and cultured; they always go on to complete
their natural growth to the same roughly 50 doublings. Cells can be isolated in

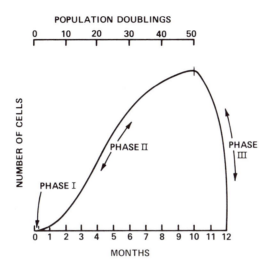

FIGURE 4-2.
Growth characteristics of human embryo fibroblast cultures in the laboratory. Phase I represents the initial growth period of fibroblast cells in the first flask. This is followed by a period of vigorous cell proliferation, Phase II, and finally a period when the cells stop dividing, Phase III. The onset of Phase III occurs at about 50 population doublings. (Redrawn with permission from L. Hayflick and P. S. Moorhead, "The Serial Cultivation of Human Diploid Cell Strains," *Experimental Cell Research* 1961, 25:585.)

one laboratory, frozen, and sent to other laboratories. One of the strains, WI-38, has been extensively studied in many places, always with similar results.

What is the relationship between the senescence of cells in a laboratory flask and the aging process in a human? It is certainly not a direct one. Hayflick and many other researchers have repeatedly emphasized that it is unlikely that animals age simply because their individual cells lose the capacity to reproduce. Indeed, certain important cells, such as nerve and muscle cells, do not divide in adult life, and yet they still show signs of deterioration with age. And changes at the subcellular level begin to be detectable in the Hayflick cultures long before the cells reach the growth limit; some of these are listed in Table 4-1. As we noted, division of cells in the human body is relatively normal in old age; centenarians still heal cuts, so their fibroblasts must still be capable of division. The aging of animals and humans more likely results from functional changes within the cells, culminating in loss of organ function, rather than simply from inability

TABLE 4-1.
Changes in Fibroblasts Growing in Tissue Culture

Parameters that increase	
Lipid synthesis	Activity of RNAase
Heat lability of G6PD	Activity of DNAase
Acid phosphatase	RNA turnover
Lysosomal enzymes	Population doubling time
Endoplasmic reticulum	cAMP level
Cytoplasmic microfibrils	Glycogen content

Parameters that decrease	
Glycolytic enzymes	Alkaline phosphatase
Pentose phosphate shunt	Number of cells proliferating
Collagen synthesis	Ribosmal RNA content
DNA synthesis	Lactate dehydrogenase
Nucleic acid synthesis	HLA specificities

Source: L. Hayflick, "The Cell Biology of Human Aging." *New England Journal of Medicine* 1976, 295:1302–1308.

to divide. The Hayflick limit or its direct analog is probably never reached during the life of an individual.

Nevertheless, several lines of evidence suggest that the Hayflick observations, if not taken too literally, can serve as a model for aging in animals and humans. The data in Table 4-2 show, for instance, that the average Hayflick limit for cells isolated from adults is less than half of the limit for fetal cells. In this experiment, the growth of fibroblasts isolated from lungs of three-month-old human fetuses was compared with adult lung fibroblasts. Fetal cells entered Phase III after 35 to 63 doublings, whereas adult cells lasted only 14 to 29 doublings before senescence. In another laboratory, Martin, Sprague, and Epstein (1970) studied 100 normal subjects of varying ages, culturing skin fibroblasts obtained from skin biopsies. There was a decrease of about 0.2 cell doublings per year of age between 10 and 90 years of age. Schneider (1976) showed that 24 elderly donors (ages 63 to 92) of skin biopsies had fibroblasts entering Phase III significantly sooner than did 23 young donors (ages 21 to 36). Although some criticisms of these studies can be raised, they establish reasonably well the inverse correlation between age of donor and number of remaining cell doublings.

A second line of evidence involves cultures taken from individuals with diseases with features of premature aging. Patients with diabetes, progeria, and

TABLE 4-2.
A Comparison of the Passage Levels at Which Phase III Occurred in Human Cells of Different Ages

Fetal Lung		Adult Lung		
Strain	Number of population doublings	Strain	Number of population doublings	Age of donor
WI-1	51	WI-1000	29	87
WI-3	35	WI-1001	18	80
WI-11	57	WI-1002	21	69
WI-16	44	WI-1003	24	67
WI-18	53	WI-1004	22	61
WI-19	50	WI-1005	16	58
WI-23	55	WI-1006	14	58
WI-24	39	WI-1007	20	26
WI-25	41			
WI-26	50			
WI-27	41			
WI-38	48			
WI-44	63			
Average	48		20	
range	(35–63)		(14–29)	

All strains were cultivated at 1:2 split ratio. Fetal strains were derived from donors of 3–4 months' gestation obtained by surgical abortion. Adult and fetal strains were derived from both male and female tissue.

Source: L. Hayflick, "The Limited in Vitro Lifetime of Human Diploid Cell Strains." *Experimental Cell Research* 1965, 37:614–636.

Werner's syndrome have decreased life spans, show many aging phenomena prematurely, and have a lower Hayflick limit—their cultured cells do not divide as many times.

A final line of evidence comes from the performance of these same experiments for different species. Table 4-3 summarizes such experiments. In general, the length of the longest line and the number of cell doublings are correlated. For example, Goldstein (1974) demonstrated that fibroblasts from four Galapagos tortoises, which may live to approximately 175 years of age, reach the Hayflick limit after 90 to 130 cell doublings. Although it is tempting to speculate that aging in the bottle and in life are the same, the data remain too fragmentary to allow such assertions. Stanley (1975), Lints (1978), and other investigators have found this relationship to be much less reliable than was originally thought.

TABLE 4-3.
Maximum Doubling Numbers and Maximum Species Life Span

Species	Maximum life span (years)	Maximum doubling number
Galapagos tortoise	175	125
Man	110	60
Horse	46	82
Chicken	30	35
Cat	28	92
Kangaroo	16	46
Mink	10	34
Mouse	4	28

Source: L. Hayflick, "The Cell Biology of Human Aging." *New England Journal of Medicine* 1976, 295:1302–1308, and J. F. Stanley, D. Pye, and A. MacGregor, "A Comparison of Doubling Numbers Attained by Cultured Animal Cells with Life Span of Species." *Nature,* 1975, 255:158–159.

The meaning of these experiments has been a subject of major controversy. Kirkwood and Holliday (1975), for example, recently proposed an ingenious explanation of the Hayflick phenomenon, which was termed the *commitment theory* of aging. This theory sees the Hayflick data as an artifact of the experimental design. The theory assumes that initially all cells in the culture are "uncommitted" and potentially immortal. Upon division, such a cell may give rise to other uncommitted cells, committed cells, or both, as shown in Figure 4-3. The committed cells are mortal; they will undergo senescence after an additional number of divisions, and, after dividing, they can give rise only to additional committed cells. Uncommitted cells, as they divide again, can again yield either committed or uncommitted cells. Since it is impossible to save all the tissue culture cells through 50 doublings (this would require many millions of flasks), the commitment theory suggests that fibroblast cells appear mortal and undergo senescence only because all the potentially immortal cells are eventually discarded. Early support for this formulation by Kirkwood and Holliday has been eroded by later work—for example, that of Harley (1980) and of Smith (1980)—which found contradictory data. WI-38 cells have been cultured in hundreds of laboratories worldwide. If this commitment theory were true, at last one uncommitted cell should have been seen. None ever has.

More substantial criticisms come from Bell and coworkers (1978), who interpret the observed changes as differentiation of cells rather than as aging. They

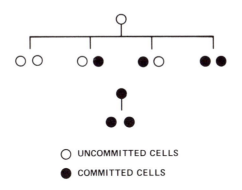

○ UNCOMMITTED CELLS

● COMMITTED CELLS

FIGURE 4-3.
The commitment theory suggests that the immortal uncommitted fibroblast cells divide to form either mortal committed cells or immortal uncommitted cells, which are discarded during serial culture transfers. This theory now has little support—no immortal cells have ever been found.

point out that the cells do not die, at least for some time—they merely fail to divide. These researchers hypothesize that the intracellular changes are those of differentiation for a particular function and do not represent senescence. Counterarguments to Bell have been offered by Hornsby and Gill (1980), and the ferment goes on. Nerve and muscle cells remain viable, even though nondividing, over quite some period; hence the distinction between cessation of cell reproduction and cell death is an important one.

Other criticisms have also been raised to the Hayflick interpretations. Addition of corticosteroids to the culture media increases the number of doublings by 20% to 30%, leading some to suspect that, with perfect culture techniques, the Hayflick limit might never be reached. And, in living organisms, it appears that the Hayflick limit would be reached only long after the species life span.

We do not believe that apparent aging in tissue culture is directly analogous to actual aging. But work in this field has helped focus further investigation indicating the importance of events at the cellular and molecular levels and the probable absence of direct central control over aging of the entire organism.

Other neglected observations further suggest finite life spans for some cellular and molecular events. For example, Siegel and his coworkers (1979) have studied lysyl oxidase, an enzyme important to the building of collagen, the connective tissue that holds our bodies together. In experiments, the forming of collagen cross-links builds for a time and then inexplicably declines. Collagen and the fibroblasts that make collagen may be critical to the aging process.

MOLECULAR AGING

Aging is thus a very complex process. Various cells, organs, and connective tissues age at different rates. Some organ systems are more critically impaired by aging than others. Susceptibility to disease processes is undoubtedly related to the aging of defense mechanisms against disease. Underlying the aging of defense mechanisms are molecular changes occurring within the cells. Ultimately we may understand aging and mortality at its most fundamental level, the molecular level. At the risk of increasing the complexity of the overall picture we have of aging, it is important to discuss what we know and don't know about molecular aging.

Information in cells is stored in code on DNA molecules. Portions of this information are transferred to RNA molecules, and instructions are carried elsewhere in the cell by this messenger RNA, which then controls the production of the particular protein involved (Figure 4-4). The protein may be a hormone, an antibody, an enzyme, or any other critical body constituent. So, protein synthesis, which underlies life, depends on the breaking, joining, migration, and correct coding of these complex molecules. If Murphy's law ("If anything can go wrong, it will") actually operates, here is a great opportunity for it. One early theory of molecular aging suggests that we deteriorate because of random critical errors in the pathway from DNA to RNA to protein.

This "error catastrophe" theory holds that random errors in the chain of protein synthesis lead inevitably to a rapid decline in cell function after a long period of good function. In a sense, this theory is related to the other dominant theory, that of a genetic clock programmed for decay and built into the DNA. In 1952, before the discovery of the structure of DNA, Medawar suggested that cell deterioration results from the "switching on" of late-acting harmful genes, but he did not specify whether a random error or a genetic clock was responsible for turning on the switch. In 1959, Szilard suggested that aging results from "random hits" that inactivate chromosomes. When a chromosome (a long strand of DNA carrying genetic information) suffers an aging "hit"—for example, from background radiation—it ceases to function if its opposite chromosome has already suffered a similar hit or has a genetic defect. The theory predicts that death of the intact organism will occur within a short time after the number of surviving somatic cells has decreased below a certain critical limit. Since two hits per cell are required, and since hits are assumed to be random, many, many hits would occur before the second hits began to occur in significant number. So, this theory

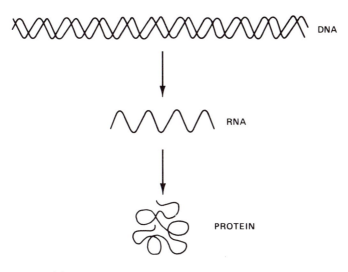

FIGURE 4-4.
Errors in the pathway of protein synthesis may lead to cell
senescence.

predicts a long period of well-being followed by a short period of rapid decay.
In a sense, this theory is an "error" theory, with the errors occurring at the level
of somatic mutations in DNA. It is not widely accepted today.

In 1963, Orgel extended this theory by suggesting that the errors could come
in the transcription of DNA into RNA or, more likely, through errors in the
translation of RNA into proteins. He proposed that random errors occurring in
the synthesis of information-carrying proteins would lead to a cascade of other
errors, with resultant cell deterioration. In other words, inaccurate protein synthesis would lead to an "error catastrophe."

In 1970, Orgel modified his own hypothesis to indicate that only errors of
sufficient magnitude and frequency would lead to catastrophe. Orgel's central
idea is that certain errors may result in further errors, and a cycle may be started
that results in death of the cell. Errors in protein synthesis lead to further errors
of protein synthesis, and the random nature of the error process is followed by
an inevitable catastrophe.

This hypothesis remains unproven experimentally. Despite serious efforts by
Hirsch (1980) and others in a number of laboratories to detect errors at the
protein level, none has yet been found. But if these models are taken very

generally, they do make sense from theoretical evolutionary viewpoints. The process of natural selection has been going on for a long time. If there were no errors, there would be no mutations, and there would be no evolution. Evolution of species is dependent, in a perverse way, on errors. If everything always worked perfectly, species could not change and improve. In evolutionary terms, the changes resulting from random molecular errors have resulted in organisms with improved chances for reproduction and survival in a changing environment. The irony is that the very error-prone mechanisms that resulted in the evolution of species may also be similar to those responsible for aging. Although plausible, these evolutionary arguments remain tenuous and without experimental confirmation.

Some other error theories are also possible. For example, there is evidence that some repair enzymes act to restore integrity of DNA. Errors could occur with these enzymes as well as in the protein synthesis sequence itself.

A final word about the cancer cell: Some of these cells are truly immortal, like the precursors of the sperm and the egg. They may be cultured in the bottle as long as desired, and they act without control in the host. Why are they not susceptible to "error catastrophe"? In theory, they may just have a lower frequency of errors, thus avoiding the catastrophe.

We have come to a paradox in our current knowledge of aging processes. For a somatic cell to become immortal, it must first become malignant. Such cell lines can divide forever, but in vivo only at the cost of consuming the organism that supports them. To live forever, a cell must kill its host, and when it kills its host, it dies. The ideal parasite, whether it be virus, bacterium, or worm, must adapt to its host at less than lethal virulence. In this sense, cancer cells are maladaptive; their actions are self-harming. The solution to human aging seems unlikely to be through changing our cells to act more like cancer cells.

The convergence of the arguments developed in this chapter should be emphasized. The best-substantiated theories of aging—at cellular, subcellular, or organ levels—point to a long period of stable function, then a rapid decline. Although some individual organ functions may decline linearly, the decline in vitality of the whole organism is exponential, as the many factors combine in a final rapid progression. The shape of this curve, with its long period of stability followed by a decline, is rectangular.

But the Deacon swore (as Deacons do,
With an "I dew vum," or an "I tell *yeou*")
He would build one shay to beat the taown
'N' the keounty 'n' all the kentry raoun';
It should be so built that it *could n'* break daown.

CHAPTER FIVE

THE
ELIMINATION OF
PREMATURE DISEASE

wherein a dramatic medical and social success story
is seen to have changed our world

Premature death in the United States has
nearly been eliminated, and its passing has hardly been noted. Sometimes progress occurs in such small steps and workers are so close to the problem that they
don't realize the task is just about finished. This chapter is about that success and
about our movement to a new era of human history. Our society has almost
eliminated premature death, and the implications for how we live and die are
momentous.

Conventional sources of information constantly emphasize the remaining
problems. We hear of an "epidemic" of lung cancer in women. An outbreak of
rabies in animals is reported in New Mexico. Gonorrhea is observed to be
increasingly common and to appear at ever younger ages. Individuals are struck
down by mysterious maladies and die despite heroic efforts to save them. The
adverse effects of our environment on our health are continually emphasized.
Entirely new diseases, such as Legionnaire's disease or Lyme disease, are still
being discovered. Clearly, these factual reports demonstrate that we still have
illness in our society, but emphasizing the exceptions obscures the rule.

After 90% or more of a problem has been eliminated, it seems reasonable to anticipate that either a complete solution to the problem is at hand or the law of diminishing returns is about to take effect. Either way, it is a good time to step back and look at the sweep of historical change, tabulate the progress, and consider future strategies. The twentieth century serves as a convenient framework for review of these dramatic events.

In developing our arguments, we have chosen to use "years of life" or "years of good health" as appropriate statistics. Implicitly, this is another way of saying that it is a greater health benefit to prevent an infant death than it is to successfully remove a cancer from a 75-year-old individual. Both are important occurrences, but in discussing national health, those factors that improve life in the early years have greater impact than those that improve life near its close. We will talk a good deal about death rates and the duration of life, in large part because the available data are precise and convincing. Morevoer, we will see in Chapter Seven that there is a close link between the quality of life and its duration, particularly with chronic disease, and we will argue strongly that the same phenomena are occurring with the quality of life as with its duration, even though the data that measure life's quality are not as precise as one might wish.

THE DECLINE IN INFECTIOUS DISEASE

Tuberculosis serves as a rather typical example of changes in health in the United States in the twentieth century. In 1840, tuberculosis was the leading cause of death in the United States, and in 1900 it was only slightly behind cardiovascular disease. Moreover, tuberculosis affected individuals earlier in life than did the diseases of the heart, hence the number of years of life lost due to tuberculosis was higher than that of any other disease at the turn of the century. In 1900, the death rate from tuberculosis was 194 per 100,000 individuals per year (Figure 5-1). By 1925, the death rate had declined by half; by 1940, by half again; by 1950, by half again; by 1955, by half again; by 1960, by half again; and again by half in 1970. In sum, mortality from tuberculosis has decreased over 99% in this century! Because of an additional shift of tuberculosis into older age groups, the number of years of life shortened by tuberculosis has decreased by 99.5%!

This incredible drop in the death rate from tuberculosis was due to many factors. Pasteurization of milk, inspection of cattle, reduction in urban overcrowding, improvement in national nutrition, isolation of cases, and other factors all

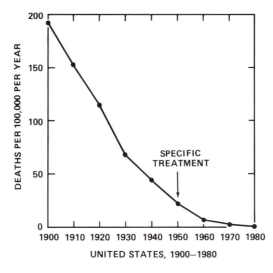

FIGURE 5-1.
The decline in death rate from tuberculosis in the
United States in the twentieth century. (From United
States Health Statistics.)

contributed importantly to the decline. Epidemiologists are fond of pointing out
that about nine-tenths of the present improvement had occurred even before we
had any drugs that would kill the tuberculosis germ. Streptomycin was the first
such drug, and it was first used in the late 1940s. Other drugs were developed
during the 1950s and 1960s. However, there is no doubt that availability of these
drugs allowed us to consolidate the previous gains, to treat difficult cases, to
greatly shorten and often eliminate hospitalizations, and to achieve a continued
decline in the death rate from this disease.

By pointing out the many factors that contributed to the decline of tuberculosis, we do not mean to imply that medical advances in antituberculous agents
were not important. They were crucial and continue to be crucial to our present
control of the disease. And the combination of measures that have successfully
eliminated the disease must be kept in force. Tuberculosis could return to this
society under some circumstances. Indeed, some low-income urban ghettos still
contain significant numbers of individuals with tuberculosis. But we understand
the means of its control, and continued vigilance will assure that we maintain
the progress we have made.

The United States Department of Public Health commonly publishes statistics on the major causes of death. Fourteen categories include almost all causes of death and serve to summarize past trends and current status. Of the fourteen categories, there have been spectacular mortality declines in nine. Six of these are now officially listed as zero mortality, meaning that their occurrence as a cause of death is now less than one in every 200,000 individuals every year (Figure 5-2). Smallpox is gone entirely. Paralytic polio, diphtheria, tetanus, typhoid and paratyphoid fevers, and whooping cough have been reduced to negligible levels. Deaths from measles and from streptococcal infections have been eliminated, even though the diseases themselves still occur. Most of these diseases disappeared because of social changes, public health measures, and immunizations. The beneficial effects of curative medical treatment are most obvious with syphilis, which declined dramatically only after the discovery of penicillin and its eventual distribution beginning about 1945. Death from syphilis is today almost entirely limited to the older individual who developed the disease before the antibiotic era, and thus syphilis deaths are now rapidly disappearing. All these conditions have declined over 99%, and in some cases, 100%!

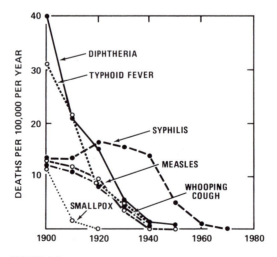

FIGURE 5-2.
The decline in death rate from some acute infectious diseases. (From United States Health Statistics.)

The only exception to the virtually complete eradication of major infectious diseases is the category of pneumonia/influenza. Here the reduction has been only 85%. However, this statistic hides an equally dramatic result. Pneumonia and influenza deaths now occur almost exclusively among the infirm, very old, or already ill. Such deaths, attributed to a germ, in fact result from diminished defense mechanisms and lost organ reserve. Deaths from these conditions in otherwise healthy individuals in the early and middle years of life have declined by the same 99% as the other infectious diseases. The actual data documenting the disappearance of major infectious diseases are listed in Table 5-1.

TABLE 5-1.
Death Rates in the United States (per 100,000 individuals)

Infectious diseases	1900	1920	1920	1930	1940	1950	1960	1970
Tuberculosis	914	154	113	71	46	23	6	2
Syphilis	13	14	17	16	14	5	2	.02
Typhoid	31	22	8	5	1	.1	0	
Streptococcal	11	11	5	2	.5	.2	.1	0
Diphtheria	40	21	15	5	1	.3	0	0
Whooping cough	12	12	11	5	2	1	.1	0
Measles	13	12	9	3	.5	.3	.2	0
Smallpox	12	1	.1	0	0	0	0	0
Pneumonia/ flu	202	156	207	102	70	31	37	31

Violent deaths								
Motor vehicles	0	2	10	27	26	23	21	27
Suicide	10	15	10	16	14	11	11	12

Chronic diseases								
Cardio/renal	345	372	365	414	486	511	522	496
Diabetes	11	15	16	19	27	16	17	19
Cancer	64	76	83	97	120	140	140	163

Source: *Historical Statistics of the United States,* Part I. U.S. Dept. of Commerce, Bureau of the Census, 1976.

THE SHIFTING THREAT TO HEALTH

With the elimination of the acute conditions, there has been a shift in the recorded causes of death to other illness categories (Figure 5-3). We will describe
the background of the emergence of chronic disease in Chapter Seven. Here, let
us note only that deaths from diseases of the heart and circulation and the various
forms of cancer have shown the largest increases as causes of death in this
century. Diseases of the heart and circulation now account for over half of all
deaths, and cancers account for about half of the remainder. The major reason
for this increase is not an epidemic; rather, it is a result of the success in virtually

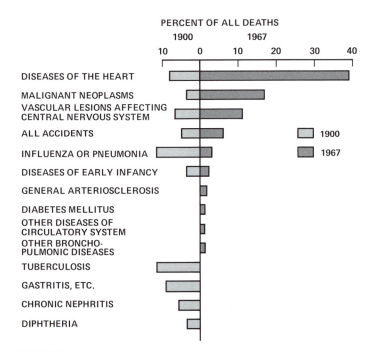

FIGURE 5-3.
Changing pattern of mortality in the United States. (Redrawn with
permission from Donabedian et al., *Medical Care Chartbook*, Fifth
Edition, Bureau of Public Health Economics, University of Michigan
School of Public Health, 1972.)

eliminating infectious diseases. Survival from the illnesses that used to kill early in life allowed the illnesses that occur later in life to increase in frequency as a cause of death.

Figure 5-4 shows the major illness categories that have not declined. Among them, a new major cause of death has appeared in this century that is of considerable interest. In 1900, there were no motor vehicles and no deaths from motor vehicle accidents. But the rate of accidental death increased substantially as more and more people drove automobiles; motor vehicle accidents now rank third nationally as a cause of death. Even more importantly, such accidental deaths occur mostly at young ages. Their effect on decreasing the quality and quantity of life is nearly equivalent to cardiovascular disease in terms of years of life affected.

As Figure 5-5 clearly shows, accidental and violent deaths are concentrated in the younger age ranges. Accidental and violent deaths constitute three-quarters of all deaths between the ages of 15 and 25 and over half of all deaths occurring prior to age 45. This is a far more important "epidemic" than any cancer. These deaths do not fit our traditional concept of illness, but they clearly play a major role in our concept of health. Violent death is the only numerically important cause of death in the United States at the present time that is not a chronic disease. All acute diseases taken together, excluding such violent deaths, have declined more than 98% over the first 80 years of this century!

THE NEED FOR A CHANGE IN THE CONVENTIONAL WISDOM

The health lore of a society is passed down from generation to generation within family units, and American health habits reflect the way things were rather than the way things are. Cultural taboos against eating with unwashed hands and sharing toothbrushes reflect a time when contagious illnesses were a major problem. School health authorities still send home children trivially ill with colds, reflecting an earlier time when the mortality rate from measles and some other acute childhood infections was significant and could be influenced by isolation measures. Such sayings as "don't go out in the cold, you will catch your death of pneumonia" are so deeply ingrained that any attempt to convince the holder of such opinions that the exposure does not constitute a health threat is usually unrewarding.

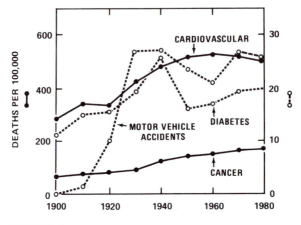

FIGURE 5-4.
Increased mortality rates from chronic diseases and
automobile accidents. (From United States Health
Statistics.)

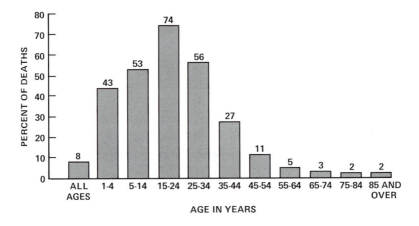

FIGURE 5-5.
Percentage of deaths attributed to accidents, homicide, and suicide according to
age in the United States, 1976. (National Center for Health Statistics, Division of
Vital Statistics.)

The media's requirement for news and our natural desire to hear of dramatic occurrences have reinforced our beliefs that acute illness continually lies in wait for each of us. The term *epidemic* often appears in the news media in a vastly exaggerated sense for sensational purposes. Sometimes an individual reports an exaggerated story; sometimes a reporter emphasizes a dramatic but otherwise insignificant event. In other instances, a public health official may use scare tactics in reaction to a small blip on the monthly statistical curves, or researchers emphasize the importance of their own particular disease interest. Sometimes, well-meaning fund-raising organizations dedicated to the control of a disease make public appeals emphasizing the dire public threat posed by their particular disease.

In contrast, there have been no major voices calling attention to the most fundamental shift in health ever to occur in the history of the human species. The figures are presented in this chapter, and there is no controversy about their accuracy. Most people no longer even know anyone with tuberculosis or small-pox or polio or typhoid fever. The only contact most of us have with diphtheria and tetanus and whooping cough is when we immunize our children against these conditions. Acute infectious illnesses and their huge contribution to the national mortality and morbidity rates are nearly gone. Barring a nuclear holo-caust, a worldwide famine, or a national social disruption, these illnesses will not recur in developed countries. Now our society must find ways to meet the challenges of chronic illness.

And that's the reason, beyond a doubt,
That a chaise *breaks down,* but doesn't *wear out.*

CHAPTER SIX

THE SHARP DOWNSLOPE
OF NATURAL DEATH

*wherein the end of a natural human life is observed
to be fixed at an average of 85 years, even without disease*

When you strip away the covering layers, the true shape of the object underneath begins to be discerned more clearly. Economic and social progress in the developing countries in this century has had the effect of slowly stripping away the effects of poverty, malnutrition, periodic famine, and infectious disease on the human life span. Observation of this progress gives us the opportunity for insights into human mortality that were denied previous societies, who saw instead a very obscured picture of natural human life and death.

The elimination of premature disease in the United States in this century is reflected in the sequence of human survival curves shown in Figure 6-1. At the 50th percentile, it is obvious that the median age at death is higher for each period; people are living longer and longer. But far more important is the change in the shape of the curve. In 1840, deaths occurred at a nearly constant rate throughout the natural life span after a high death rate in the first year. In 1900, there was still a high rate of infant mortality, but the curve was beginning to bend

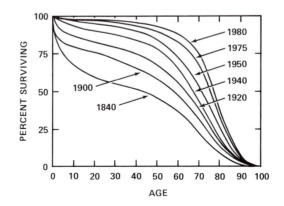

FIGURE 6-1.
Sequential survival curves in the United States. The progressive elimination of premature death allows these curves to begin to approximate the curve that would be found in the absence of any premature death. (U.S. Bureau of Health Statistics.)

slightly upward. At later periods, the first part of the curve becomes flatter and flatter, and the last part of the curve becomes steeper and steeper. The curves for all years converge at about the same point, with very little difference among eras as we reach the tail of the survival curve. The curve is becoming rectangular. The ever-sharper downslope represents the barrier to immortality; it represents graphically the upper limit of the natural human life span.

We emphasize that these data are highly accurate and incontrovertible. The National Bureau of Health Statistics has kept precise vital statistics for the United States throughout this period. Prior to 1932, data were drawn from the so-called registration states, and thereafter from the entire population, with a present base of over 200 million persons. There is no question that the striking phenomenon of rectangularization of the survival curve has been occurring and that it is nearly complete.

IMPLICATIONS OF THE RECTANGULAR CURVE

The rectangular curve is a critical concept, and its implications affect each of our lives. The rectangular curve is not a rectangle in the absolute sense, nor will it ever be. The changing shape of the curve results from both biological and environmental factors. Many biological phenomena describe what is often called a normal distribution. This is the familiar bell-shaped or Gaussian curve. If one studies the ages at death in a well-cared-for and relatively disease-free animal population, one finds that their ages at death are distributed on both sides of an average age of death, with the number of individuals becoming less frequent in both directions as one moves farther from the average age at death. A theoretical distribution of ages at death taking the shape of such a curve in humans is shown in Figure 6-2. This simple bell-shaped curve, with a mean of 85 years and a standard deviation of 4 years, might exemplify the age at death of an ideal, disease-free, violence-free human society. The sharp downslope of the bell-shaped survival curve is analogous to the sharp downslope of the rectangular curve.

In Figure 6-1, the first part of the curve becomes ever flatter, reflecting lower rates of infant mortality. Several factors prevent the total elimination of infant mortality and thus prevent the curve from becoming perfectly horizontal. These premature deaths are the result of birth of defective babies, premature disease, and violent death. Improvements in medicine can lower but never eliminate the birth of defective babies and premature disease. It seems likely that the ever

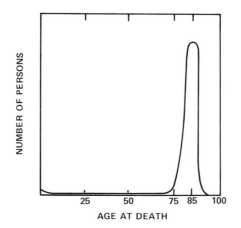

FIGURE 6-2.
Ideal mortality curve in the absence of premature death. The average death occurs at age 85, with a standard deviation of about 4 years. Ninety-five percent of all deaths occur between the ages of 77 and 93. (U.S. Bureau of Health Statistics.)

dominant proportion of violent deaths during early life will prove recalcitrant to change and will form an ever larger fraction of total premature deaths.

So, the rectangular curve has an initial brief, steep downturn because of deaths shortly after birth, a very slow rate of decline through the middle years, a relatively abrupt turn to a very steep downslope as one nears the age of death of the ideal Gaussian curve, and a final flattening of the curve as the normal biological distribution of deaths results in a tail after the age of 90.

Statisticians and government agencies often talk about average values and pay rather less attention to the individual distributions about those values. Hence, the public perception of changes in survival curves is represented by the curves shown earlier in Figure 1-1. If we explain the concept of a survival curve to students and ask them to draw survival curves as they have changed in this century, they usually draw a set of curves very much like those of Figure 1-1. They draw the curves that might result if man were potentially immortal. An increase in life expectancy at any age in such curves is paralleled by an increase in life expectancy at every other age. If the average age at death rose by 25 years, so would the oldest age at death rise 25 years.

Thus, two profound characteristics of the mortality of man, the elimination of premature disease and the development of the sharp downslope representing natural death, have remained far from the public consciousness. These data have been available for many years. The first solid comments about rectangularization of the human survival curve can be found in prophetic statements in the 1920s. Many statisticians and actuaries working with national health data since that time have noted the increasingly rectangular shape of the curve, and many have speculated that it represents a natural species life limit. Entire theories of the aging process, as noted in previous chapters, have been built around the observed fact of a natural life span in man and animals. Yet, the public has remained largely ignorant of these developments.

A society in which life expectancy is believed to increase at every age and in which one becomes increasingly feeble as one grows older is a society heading for trouble. A society moving according to the curves of Figure 6-1, as our society is, is a society moving toward a world in which there is little or no disease, and individuals live out their natural life span fully and vigorously, with a brief terminal period of infirmity. These social implications will be discussed later; here we intend to indicate their origin. Dramatic changes in mortality patterns result in equally dramatic social changes.

THE IDEAL HUMAN LIFE SPAN

We can now calculate the ideal human life span. As we extend the curves of Figure 6-1 yet a few more layers, we reach the top curve of Figure 6-3. The resulting natural or "ideal" curve has an average age at death of 85 years. With the assumption that violent death will remain, the ideal curve will have a slow early decline, with the form shown in the figure. The precise shape and location of this curve may be calculated statistically in several ways, using existing knowledge of mortality trends and the knowledge of the limits to the life span already discussed. Figures 6-4 and 6-5 provide data for such calculations.

Since 1900, we have already progressed the great majority of the distance, in terms of years of life saved, toward this ideal curve. Disregarding traumatic and violent death, progress in eliminating premature death since 1900 has, by 1980, removed about 80% of the area between the ideal curve and the 1900 curve. Moreover, the greatest change has occurred in the earlier years of life; most remaining premature death is concentrated in the years over age 60 and is due to the chronic illnesses discussed in the next chapter.

These changes are dramatic. In 1900, the average individual died 38 years prematurely. In 1950, the average individual died 17 years prematurely; in 1980,

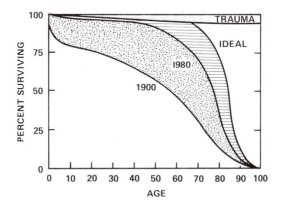

FIGURE 6-3.
Ideal survival curve resulting from the elimination of premature disease in the United States. By 1980, over 80% of the area between the curve for 1900 and the ideal curve had been reduced. (U.S. Bureau of Health Statistics.)

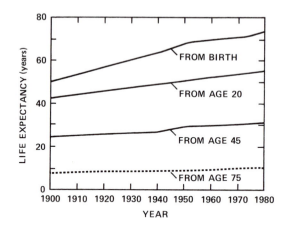

FIGURE 6-4.
Change in life expectancy in the United States during the twentieth century. From birth, life expectancy has risen from 47 years to 73 years. In contrast, from age 75, the increase has been only from 8 years to 11 years. The greater the age from which life expectancy is calculated, the less has been the improvement. (U.S. Bureau of Health Statistics.)

the average individual died only 12 years prematurely. White females in 1980 died on the average only 7 years short of the theoretical limit. And, of the remaining years of average premature death, 3 of these years are accounted for by violent death. Clearly, the medical and social task of eliminating premature death, from this point of view, is largely accomplished.

Another way to look at the natural life span is to consider trends in life expectancy. This is a slightly different statistical representation and is shown in Figure 6-4. The average length of life in the United States has increased from approximately 47 years at the turn of the century to over 73 years today, an increase of more than 25 years. Life expectancy for white females is now 78 years, and for white males, 70 years. The steady rise in life expectancy in the early years of this century changed to a relative plateau after about 1950, but the rise has resumed over the past 6 or 7 years. These data, shown as the top line of Figure 6-4, are familiar to many, and they serve as the basis for predictions about the increasing numbers of individuals over age 65 in our population as the result of previous "baby booms" and for often erroneous projections of the type and number of medical facilities likely to be required in the future.

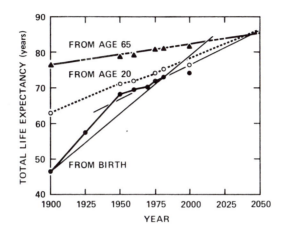

FIGURE 6-5.
Projected estimates of life expectancy in the United States. The lines representing
improvement in life expectancy at different ages can be extrapolated into the future to
give a maximum estimate for the natural life span in the absence of premature death.
Here projections from birth *(solid circles)* are made for the past 80 years and for the
most recent decade to indicate the similarity of the estimated life span with different
assumptions. The life span is approximated by the points of intersections with
projections from age 65 *(solid triangles)* or age 20 *(open circles)*. Estimates from the
Office of the Actuary for the year 2000 suggest a projection slightly less than age 85.
(National Center for Health Statistics, 1977. Figures for the year 2000 are estimates
from the Office of the Actuary.)

    A critical look at these data, however, shows that the increase in life expectancy
results from the elimination of premature death rather than by extension of the
natural life span. When life expectancy is calculated from particular ages, the
higher the age, the less is the increase. From age 40, life expectancy has increased
relatively little. From age 75, the increase is barely perceptible. Beyond the age
of 85, an increase cannot be confidently determined at all.
    A white female age 70 now has an average life expectancy of 14 years, and a
white male of the same age has a life expectancy of 11 years. Present differences
between sexes and between races become much smaller as the age on which
the analysis is based is increased. Minorities, including men, simply have more
premature death. Interestingly, above the age of 66, remaining life expectancy
for black females is greater than that for white females. Most observers believe
that the life span for blacks and whites is the same and that this unexpected

longevity in elderly black females is the result of selection of the particularly hardy by their greater resistance to injury and disease in earlier life.

A major paradox is created if we extend the lines shown in Figure 6-4 into the future. It seems reasonable to do so, since these lines have been constant in slope for the past century, and it seems reasonable to assume that they might continue so into the next century. The paradox is that, if life expectancy from birth continues to climb, there will be a date at which life expectancy from birth is higher than expected age at death calculated from age 65 or age 75. This is not possible.

These same data may be presented in a different way, and they may be used to calculate the duration of the human life span. Figure 6-5 shows that representation. With life expectancy from birth increasing at a slope of about 3/10ths of a year per year and life expectancy from age 65 increasing by about 1/20th of a year per year, the curves will intersect in the first half of the next century. Depending on the base from which one extends the projections, a variety of different projections may be obtained. When we make certain assumptions, we obtain an intersection point as low as 82.4 years, intersecting in the year 2009. Using other assumptions, we can project a high estimate of 85.6 years. The curves in Figure 6-5 represent a reasonable, average set of assumptions and intersect at age 85 in the year 2045, and the two lines drawn for the rate of increase in life expectancy from birth serve to illustrate the relatively slight effect of using quite different assumptions. Of course, in actuality the curves will not be straight. They will approach the limit more gradually as the point of diminishing returns is reached, so that the attainable life expectancy from birth will be less than the theoretical estimate of 85 years.

The data shown in Figure 6-5 for the year 2000 illustrate this point. These are the current estimates from the U.S. Office of the Actuary. It can be seen that these projections are for a slower rate of growth in life expectancy over the next two decades than has occurred earlier in this century; they are below the lines projected from past improvement. Such estimates suggest that the actual limit to the human life span may be slightly less than 85 years, and these estimates strengthen the arguments presented here.

The best projections we can develop indicate that the median natural human life span is set at a maximum of 85 years with a standard error of less than one year. Making the assumption of a biological bell-shaped distribution, and taking account of the known frequency of individuals living into their second century of life, one can calculate the standard deviation to be slightly less than 4 years.

In other words, one in 10,000 individuals reaches the age of 100; this age is approximately 4 standard deviations from the mean. By the statistical rules of normal distributions, in the ideal setting, two-thirds of natural deaths would occur between the ages of 81 and 89, and 95% of natural deaths would occur between the ages of 77 and 93.

We should mention a few uncertainties, although the arguments above do not depend on them. The human life span might not be absolutely fixed but might be slowly increasing, perhaps as much as a month or so each century. The data are consistent with the possibility of such an increase. And we would not like these estimates to be construed too literally. We will always have some illness and accidental and violent death. Man's inhumanity to man appears as fundamental a biological principle as the finite life span, and it will always prevent us from reaching the ideal. And our medical care delivery system will at some point of diminishing returns make it very hard to move farther toward the ideal life span. But, as we begin to indicate in the next chapter, we see room for major improvement with the currently leading causes of death, and we expect that the next several decades will see continued progress toward the ideal rectangular curve.

"Fur," said the Deacon, " 't's mighty plain
Thut the weakes' place mus' stan' the strain;
'N' the way t' fix it, uz I maintain,
              Is only jest
T' make that place uz strong uz the rest."

CHAPTER SEVEN

THE EMERGENCE OF CHRONIC, UNIVERSAL DISEASE

wherein the diseases of aging and of the aged
are seen to be the major challenges of human health

The nature of our health problem is clear. The strategy for the solution is almost incontrovertible. But the effects of the strategy on human aging have not been analyzed, and they are very striking effects indeed.

The major challenge to human health in developed countries lies in the so-called chronic diseases. Data demonstrating the emergence of these diseases over the course of this century were given in Chapter Five. Atherosclerosis and other arterial disease, cancer, diabetes, arthritis, emphysema, and cirrhosis cause over 80% of all premature deaths and over 90% of all disability. Obviously, no major improvement in health is possible without an attack on these disease processes.

CHRONIC DISEASE

A consideration of the nature of chronic disease underlies the strategies for improvement. There are striking parallels among the various major chronic diseases, and there are striking differences between these and the previously formidable acute diseases. There also exists a third class of major diseases, to be described, which are neither acute nor encountered by almost all individuals.

A chronic disease has characteristics far more important than duration, and definition of *chronic* in terms of time has little value. While "duration greater than six weeks" or similar expressions often have been used to define *chronic,* we suggest that more important insights come from the fact that these diseases tend to (1) be incremental, (2) be universal, (3) have a clinical threshold, and (4) be characterized by a progressive loss of organ reserve. In many ways, these diseases are similar to normal processes of gradual loss of function with age, but the disease processes cause such loss to occur at an accelerated rate.

These universal conditions (perhaps *universal* is a better term than *chronic*) begin relatively early in adult life. They begin with minor changes in the cells of a particular organ, gradually cause microscopically visible damage, continue to progress until they can be determined in presymptomatic form by various tests, and eventually emerge as disease symptoms in the patient. From this point, the process continues as a set of worsening symptomatic problems and eventually culminates in disability or death. Often the process itself begins early in adult life, with a subsequent life-long incremental progression. The most important chronic disease, atherosclerosis, serves as an example of this process (Figure 7-1).

Atheroma can be detected at autopsy following accidental death in many twenty-year-olds, and by X-ray arteriograms in many asymptomatic individuals in their thirties and forties. Both the development of atherosclerotic plaques on the inside walls of arteries and another process, the fibrous-tissue scarring of medial muscular arterial coats, begin in early adulthood. As the artery becomes narrower, and the wall itself becomes more rigid, the passage of blood becomes more difficult. Higher blood pressures may be required to force the passage, and the higher pressures may increase the rate of damage to the arterial walls. Passing platelets may adhere to the damaged areas, and clots (thrombosis) may occur, completely blocking the blood flow. If the clotted artery supplies a critical body part, death or severe symptoms may occur instantly at the time the clot forms. If the process has developed in a single location, such as the left anterior descending coronary artery (the "artery of sudden death"), then death can occur, even though the rest of the arteries are not compromised. If the process has progressed relatively evenly in many arteries, the first symptoms may be those of inadequate circulation, such as chest pain (angina pectoris), intermittent leg pain (claudication), or abdominal discomfort. Sometimes an aneurysm (bal-

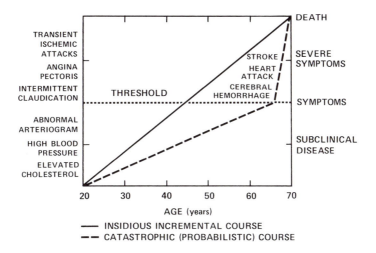

FIGURE 7-1.
The clinical course of atherosclerosis. Atherosclerosis may
progress relatively evenly, or it may result in a sudden catastrophic
event such as heart attack or stroke. Both the decrease in vessel
caliber and flow and the probability of catastrophe proceed
incrementally and progressively. The other major chronic illnesses
show similar progressions.

looning) of the aorta may cause the first symptoms, and sometimes hemorrhage
from a damaged artery into the brain is the first manifestation.

The sequence depicted in Figure 7-1 is of course greatly oversimplified. The
actual events underlying arterial degeneration are more complex and often controversial. They include development of atheromatous plaques (atherosclerosis),
high-blood-pressure-associated lesions in the smaller blood vessels (arteriolo-
sclerosis), degeneration of the medial layer of the arteries, and an increase in
fibrous tissue with a decrease in elasticity that appears to be age related.
Conceptually, however, problems with arterial reserve illustrate well the principles underlying universal incremental illness. The process long antedates the
first symptoms of disease. The clinical threshold may be passed either abruptly,
as with a heart attack or stroke, or slowly, as with the several syndromes of arterial
insufficiency and their associated pain due to oxygen starvation. As the disease
progresses, the time at which the first irreversible symptom will be felt comes
nearer, and the probability of a sudden catastrophe increases. These princi-

ples are expressed to some degree in each of the major chronic illnesses (Figure 7-2).

Unseen passage toward illness or the probability of catastrophe can be true also of diabetes, cancer, osteoarthritis, emphysema, and cirrhosis as well as numerically less important diseases of other organs. The parallel progressions are listed in Table 7-1. For example, in noninsulin-dependent (Type II) diabetes, one may initially detect elevated fasting blood glucose, then sugar in the urine, then diabetic complications of eye, nerve, and kidney. With osteoarthritis, the joint cartilage first has different staining characteristics; later, a narrowed joint space and some bone spurs can be seen on X-ray. Precancerous states show irritated and aberrant-appearing cells. The preemphysematous lung first loses some alveolar septal walls, and the patient manifests difficulty in expelling air with normal flow rates. The precirrhotic liver first enlarges, with fatty infiltration and inflammation. In each of these conditions, many people with the early stages never progress to the later stages during their lifetimes, and many people do not progress smoothly through all these stages. But the conditions, often influenced by environmental or self-induced insults to the organ, can be considered

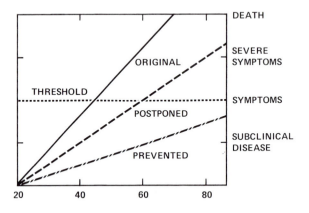

FIGURE 7-2.
The clinical course of chronic disease. The universal, chronic diseases begin early in life, progress through a clinical threshold, and eventuate in disability or death. An important strategy for their control is to alter the rate (slope) at which they develop, thus postponing the clinical illness or even "preventing" it.

TABLE 7-1.
The Increments of Chronic Disease

Age	Stage	Atherosclerosis	Cancer	Osteoarthritis	Diabetes	Emphysema	Cirrhosis
20	start	elevated cholesterol	carcinogen exposure	abnormal cartilage staining	obesity	smoker	drinker
30	discernible	small plaques on arteriogram	cellular metaplasia	slight joint space narrowing	abnormal glucose tolerance	mild airway obstruction	fatty liver on biopsy
40	subclinical	larger plaques on arteriogram	increasing metaplasia	bone spurs	elevated fasting blood glucose	X-ray hyperinflation	enlarged liver
50	threshold	leg pain on exercise	carcinoma in situ	mild articular pain	sugar in urine	shortness of breath	upper GI hemorrhage
60	severe	angina pectoris	clinical cancer	moderate articular pain	hypoglycemic drug requirement	recurrent hospitalization	ascites
70	end	stroke, heart attack	metastatic cancer	disabled	blindness; neuropathy; nephropathy	intractable oxygen debt	jaundice; hepatic coma

schematically to be universal. Only the rate of their development is different in different people.

Each of these conditions manifests accelerated loss of organ reserve—in the arteries, the joint cartilage, the lungs, the liver, and the organs that are the sites of the various cancers. These are the major illnesses of our day.

Some important, long-lasting diseases do not have these characteristics and constitute a third group of conditions which are neither acute nor universal. Examples of these are Hodgkin's disease, ulcerative colitis, insulin-dependent (Type I) diabetes, rheumatoid arthritis, psoriasis, multiple sclerosis, muscular dystrophy, and schizophrenia. These conditions are not universal, they are not incremental in the same sense, and they act much more like acute illnesses. That is, it often seems as though you may "catch" them, they spontaneously disappear on occasion, they may reverse impressively after medication or operation, or in some instances they may even be cured. These conditions do not parallel the natural aging process, and thus they are not included in our classification of chronic, universal diseases. Arteriosclerosis is hard to classify, as it is not universal in all countries. Arterial degeneration, referring broadly to loss of elasticity in the vessel wall and development of fibrotic change, probably is a universal condition.

This distinction between chronic, universal conditions and other long-lasting diseases is critical, even though it is arbitrary; some would classify certain diseases differently than would others. Regardless of classification differences, three points hold: (1) The universal diseases are by far the greatest current health problem in the United States. (2) The best strategy for control of the chronic diseases that represent accelerated aging is to attempt to slow the rate of their progression. (3) The medical tradition of searching for primary cure remains particularly appropriate for the long-lasting, but not universal, diseases.

A distinction between two types of progression of chronic diseases is also important. The progression can be either in the disease process itself or in the probability of acquiring the condition. Indeed, both types of progression can occur simultaneously. Cancer illustrates this point. From one point of view, cancer begins with a single malignant cell, becomes two cells, then four, and ultimately expands to threaten the organism. It is at first undetectable, but it passes a clinical threshold, after which it causes symptoms and then eventuates, in many cases, in death. But, from another viewpoint, the "probability" of cancer is what is universal and what progresses. Most cancers occur late in life, and the probability of occurrence increases year by year. Even if a particular cancer is cured by medication or by surgical excision, the probability of development of a second cancer relentlessly progresses with time. Many scientists believe that the immune surveillance system, which enables us to reject small cancers from our body before they become a problem, deteriorates with age, giving minor malignant changes a better chance to become serious illnesses. Others think that the rate of malignant change itself increases with time. Whatever the mechanism, the probability of an individual developing cancer increases with the years, and the cancer, once present, also enlarges with time. We intend our concept of chronic, incremental disease to include both increase in the probability of disease and increase in the disease process itself.

We do not know the aggravating or risk factors for all universal diseases, and thus we cannot assume that all such diseases may be affected by changes in environment. For example, some cancers (such as cancer of the prostate) are not reliably associated with modifiable factors. A popular current estimate is that about 50% of cancer is already known to be due to hazards in the environment, whether personal smoking, industrial pollution, alcohol, medications, coffee, or other substances. Some of the remaining 50% may be environmentally caused also, but some may not. But, the chronic diseases for which we do not strongly suspect causes in the environment or personal behavior are greatly outnumbered by those for which we do.

The major health problem, then, is universal, chronic, incremental, accelerated loss of organ reserve, under many disease guises, which we call by different names and which affect different organs. The solution is to postpone these diseases—not to "cure" them, but to slow them down. For most such diseases, we already know how to decrease the probability of occurrence, the incremental growth, or both. We have identified the risk factors, and from these we are able to formulate a strategy for better health.

STRATEGY

If we can slow the rate at which universal diseases progress, we will delay the time of their clinical appearance—that is, the time when the symptomatic threshold is passed. If we sufficiently delay this passage, symptoms will not develop during the natural life span, and the disease will have been "prevented." Actually, the disease process will not have disappeared, but its accelerated characteristics will have been lost, and, from the standpoint of the affected individual, it is as if it never occurred. Figure 7-2 shows the nature of prevention in these conditions. The process is slowed, not prevented, and the clinical threshold is postponed, not prevented. But our finite life span allows this process to appear as though it were actually preventive.

Postponement of chronic disease is accomplished by removal of risk factors associated with acceleration of the process. There are a number of well-established risk factors, and the success of this strategy has been shown with many but not all of them. The risk factors include cigarette smoking, excessive alcohol consumption, excessive body weight, excessive consumption of fatty foods, inadequate exercise, exposure to environmental toxins, inadequate use of mature psychological defense mechanisms, and living in the psychological state of helplessness, without options for major life choices and decisions. The state of our knowledge of each of these has been reviewed in detail many times; the references at the end of this volume will guide the reader to some of the most formative writings. The comments that follow are our synopsis of a large literature, and we will return to discussion of many of these factors in the next chapter in the broader context of aging rather than disease prevention.

Exercise

Exercise, performed aerobically, regularly, without pain, and relatively safely, as with walking rapidly, jogging, bicycling, or swimming, is one of the most important and positive health influences known. This type of exercise is known to increase cardiac reserve, improve pulmonary reserve, increase arterial diameter, lower serum cholesterol, increase the high-density lipoproteins, aid in weight control, improve bowel function, add bone and muscle strength, tighten ligaments, improve glucose utilization, and decrease many measures of stress. It is the key to several of the other risk factors.

Cigarette Smoking

Cigarette smoking is the most harmful of the habits to which we voluntarily submit. Its effects begin with a very few cigarettes, increase with both frequency and duration of the habit, and may be partially reversed after decreasing usage. Its causal role in lung cancer and in emphysema is definitely established, even though both conditions can also occur (uncommonly) without smoking. Smoking is an important risk factor for atherosclerosis, particularly coronary artery disease. The harmful effects can be readily induced in laboratory animals. Reports of the Surgeon General's Office summarize the available evidence, which is overwhelmingly persuasive. Danger to the nonsmoker in the same room is very much less but may be real. Smoking increases the chances for respiratory diseases by 10 to 100 times the amount that they are increased by heavy environmental smog.

Excessive Alcohol Consumption

Several recent studies have shown that moderate alcohol consumption is, if anything, healthful, and the absolute prohibitions of a few years ago are beginning to soften. Still, alcoholism is a major national problem, affecting as many as one in six individuals in certain urban locations. It causes almost all cases of cirrhosis of the liver and is associated with the majority of massive hemorrhages from the stomach or duodenum. It is the underlying cause of a large proportion of motor vehicle accidents and an equally large proportion of suicides and homicides. Alcoholics are hospitalized from three to five times as frequently as nonalcoholics and have a markedly shortened duration of life. Breslow (1979) and Valliant (1979) have reviewed much of the present evidence for harmful effects from alcohol. Indirectly, some of the harm may come from associated life failures and the resultant stresses.

Obesity

An increase in obesity poses major health problems for many individuals, although fat has survival value in societies where a regular food supply is not available. Associated states include high blood pressure, elevated serum cholesterol and other lipids, and an increased risk of Type II diabetes. Certain other diseases, such as gallbladder disease and gout, are more frequent, and surgery is more hazardous. Inactivity is often associated with being overweight, and such persons have increased stress levels and decreased feelings of self-worth as compared with others.

Diet

Many authorities are not as sure today about risk factors of diet composition (as opposed to overeating) as they were a few years ago. High cholesterol, elevated low-density lipoproteins, and decreased high-density lipoproteins are all statistical risk factors for arterial disease. They can be changed by dietary change, but each is associated with obesity, high blood pressure, and inactivity, and all of these factors are associated with each other, so it is difficult to be sure which factor is primary and which is secondary.

Environmental Toxins

There are so many possible threats to our health from our environment that we cannot discuss each thoroughly. Of the major risk factors, environmental toxins are unique in that they cannot be controlled by a single individual but require collective effort. In many cases, such as industrial exposure to asbestos, beryllium, chromate, or some other chemicals, the causal role is firmly established. In others, such as medical irradiation, saccharin, and some food dyes, the evidence is controversial. Except in a few particularly hazardous industries, the personal toxins (such as cigarette smoking) are a much greater threat to health than are environmental toxins.

Suppression

Many personal psychological mechanisms seem to affect physical health directly or indirectly. These associations are new and not yet proven, but research has progressed to the point where a discussion of risk factors cannot be limited to the biomedical factors alone. We all have a variety of defense mechanisms that we use to adapt to life crises, some of which represent psychological health and some of which are themselves pathological. One of the best known studies of these defense mechanisms, by Valliant, suggests that both physical and psychological health are enhanced by using mature defense mechanisms, particularly those that involve humor, altruism, mild denial, or suppression of the problem. Persons who are able to minimize the importance of adverse events and put their problems promptly behind them remain healthier than those who cannot.

Helplessness

Theories relating health to feelings of helplessness and frustration, particularly as developed by Seligman, indicate that these psychological states may pose severe threats to health. Some animals show increased survival, greater health, and even delayed development of cancer when raised in a environment contrived to be less frustrating as compared with litter mates raised under normal laboratory conditions. A variety of human data also suggest that better health is associated with autonomy and with control of the environment by the individual rather than control of the individual by the environment. A feeling of self-worth, a feeling of personal contribution, and a sense of personal control over the future are positively associated with good health. Some would maintain that people have these positive feelings because they are healthy, not that people are healthy because of their personal exercise of autonomy. But experiments with animals suggest the opposite, that the exercise of personal choice and the suffering of the consequence of these choices, for good or ill, are important to physical well-being.

Injury

The major acute health problem of our time is traumatic and accidental injury and death. Even here, personal risk factors dominate. Convincing evidence suggests that personal use of seat belts and other passive restraints, observance of 55 mile per hour speed limits, voluntary decrease in miles driven per year, and avoidance of driving while intoxicated or not driving at hours when others are likely to be intoxicated could eliminate most violent deaths. We would like to see these measures considered as preventive medicine rather than as nonmedical problems, and we encourage research into behavior change and incentive modification in this area as well as research into better highway design and safer vehicles.

THE ROLE OF PERSONAL CHOICE

Removal of many of these risk factors thus requires personal choice, and the very process of making the choices may itself have positive health benefits. The role of individual responsibility will be discussed at some length in Chapter Ten, but it is worth noting here that society shapes the choices of the individual. Societal incentives have often ignored health consequences, as in the subsidization of tobacco crops, in the creation of social payments that separate individuals from the consequences of their actions, and in incentives that have fostered a litigious society. We make personal choices under many influences, and society ought to be sure that individuals are encouraged to make decisions that improve health.

Moreover, concerted effort is required to minimize many of the risk factors that threaten health. Drunken driving penalties, air pollution standards, mandatory protections from toxic chemicals, and objective information sources for the consumer are part of a rational strategy to improve human health. The individual in our modern democracy has a voice and a vote but often faces powerful special-interest lobbies, so that political campaigns are often necessary to achieve even self-evident consumer improvements.

One may ask whether strategies based on behavior change and personal choice have any likelihood of success. Often we hear of disappointing results from such efforts. The failure of national antismoking campaigns, the lack of medical success with treatment of obesity, the recalcitrance of alcoholism, and the inability to change teenage driving habits are frequently cited as evidence that "you just can't change human nature." These observations, however, arise from misplaced expectations and epidemic impatience rather than from accurate analysis. The changes indeed have been slow, but signs of improvement can be seen.

For example, there have been substantial changes in smoking behavior in the fifteen years since the first Surgeon General's report on the harmful effects of cigarette smoking. Per-capital tobacco consumption is down 26%, and cigarettes with less tar and better filters account for a greater proportion of total tobacco consumption. Among the college educated and young adults, the changes have been greater. And for those closest to the data—physicians—the smokers have declined from a large majority of 79% to a small minority of 14%.

There has also been a decline of about one third in per-capital consumption of saturated fats. We have a five-pound leaner national body weight per person, despite a slight increase in the national average height. Aerobic exercise programs have been adopted in school athletic programs, and the national road-running phenomenon is too obvious to need much mention—there are now some 30 million joggers.

In making health projections, we should expect that these changes will be reflected in greater well-being, but only after the lag period required for intervention in the rate of development of universal disease. Thus, lung cancer in men should peak in frequency in the early 1980s and will then decline slowly, the decline from the peak frequency being greater than the 26% decline in per-capita cigarette smoking. Emphysema statistics should follow a similar curve. For women, the peak of the curve will be reached about five years later, but the same decline will follow. We are currently reaping the bitter harvest of "you've come a long way, baby" and it will be a few years before the present decreases are fully reflected in the frequency of disease above the threshold. At present, the decline in cigarette smoking in both men and women is accelerating, giving hope that the ultimate effect will be far greater than can be presently projected. But a 25% decrease in the two major chronic lung illnesses will represent a spectacular achievement.

With arterial disease, the situation is even better. For the first time, we have recorded improvement in a progressive universal illness. The incidence of all cardiovascular disease has declined steadily over the past decade. Age-adjusted overall ischemic heart disease mortality declined by 20% between 1968 and 1976. The decline in cerebrovascular disease, including strokes, has been the most marked, and the total decrease has been about one-quarter. There remains controversy about the cause of this great improvement, with advocates of diet, exercise, decreased cigarette smoking, and improved treatment of hypertension all willing to receive the credit. No single factor seems to explain the decline very satisfactorily, and it seems likely that a combination of influences have been important. But, the improvement is there. Change is possible.

In Chapter Nine we develop the concept of the plasticity of aging, using examples from physical activity, psychological factors, and intelligence. *Plasticity* implies that deterioration of a function with age is not preordained, except in very broad statistical terms. An individual can alter the rate of aging in most of the important variables. Here, we note in advance of that discussion that the postponement of chronic illness is a form of plasticity; it represents the ability of the individual, by personal decisions, to delay the onset of infirmity.

THE COMPRESSION OF INFIRMITY

Given the preceding definition of our major health problem, and the probable effectiveness of the remedial strategy, we can now look at the results we are likely to obtain. Most obvious is the postponement of chronic, universal illness itself. Figure 7-3 shows this phenomenon schematically for an individual. On the top line, the present crescendo of illness over a typical lifetime is portrayed. A serious disease, such as pneumonia, might occur early in adult life. If the person survives, a later illness, such as a heart attack at age 50, might occur. Survivors of such episodes move farther along their lifeline to other diseases, such as emphysema, stroke, and lung cancer. Finally, the survivors of all these illnesses reach the time of natural death.

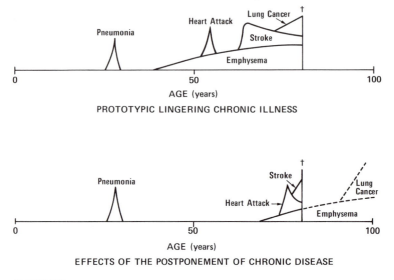

FIGURE 7-3.

The compression of morbidity. The ability to postpone chronic disease, taken together with the biological limit represented by the life span, results in the ability to shorten the period between the clinical onset of chronic disease and the end of life. Infirmity (morbidity) is compressed into a shorter and shorter period near the end of the life span.

Notice the effect of increased survival from premature illness in unmasking the later diseases. Now, the individual may have several illnesses, and they are much more likely to be chronic, expensive ones rather than brief, acute ones. Illnesses occur more frequently with age, and several may coexist at once. The exchange of acute disease for chronic and the increase in the average life expectancy have resulted in a dramatic increase in medical costs and in an increase in the number of years of impaired health per person. Lingering illness has become much more common in our society than in previous years and in previous societies.

A dramatic reversal, however, is about to occur. A phenomenon that we term the *compression of infirmity* will appear as the postponement of chronic illness continues. The central reasons for the change—the implications of the rectangular curve—have been introduced in earlier chapters. If the maximum life span is fixed, as the age at onset of illness increases, the period of illness must become shorter. Illness will then become less lingering, not more. The bottom line in Figure 7-3 shows this effect. With chronic illness delayed—in some cases, so delayed that the illness will not occur within the life span—the period of adult vigor is prolonged.

Moreover, illness at the end of the life span will prove more refractory to treatment, more inevitable, less possible to cure, and increasingly less reasonable to treat. As we evolve toward these illness patterns, we can expect an acceleration of the already visible trends toward living wills, hospices, home care, and generally more humane attention to the dying. And, if society responds to these opportunities in a rational way, we should find need for fewer medical services, less intensive care for the terminally ill, fewer hospitalization days, and decreased national medical costs.

We have emphasized the progressive nature of chronic disease for an additional purpose, to make clear that the impact of illness on the quality of life is closely linked to its impact on the duration of life. Disability precedes death, and first infirmity is linked to death over a period of slowly increasing disability. The consequences of this linkage are predictable. As the mortality curve becomes nearly rectangular, a hypothetical morbidity curve must also become more rectangular. Rectangularization of the curve representing the end of the period of adult vigor, not just the curve representing the end of life, must occur. The rectangular curve implies that living longer than the maximum species life span is not possible. But it also implies that it may be possible to live well until the end of the life span.

Figure 7-4 shows the life expectancy in 1950 and an ideal projection. This ideal curve is simply a different representation of the rectangular curve. Each curve represents a population of individuals. As the curves shift to the right, all individuals live longer. But life expectancy increases more for earlier ages than for later ages; life expectancy from age 20 increases more than does life expectancy from age 70 or 80. This shift was discussed in Chapter Six, where these data were used to calculate the ideal life span and its distribution.

Over the next decades, the difference in increase in life expectancy from birth and age 70 will not be nearly as apparent. The great majority of premature deaths now occur over the age of 60, and most occur over the age of 70. The typical individual in an ideal society would live 10 or 12 years longer than at present, and most of these additional years would be lived following age 70. So, life expectancy from age 70 will increase as chronic disease is postponed, and life expectancy from age 70 will increase almost as fast as life expectancy from age

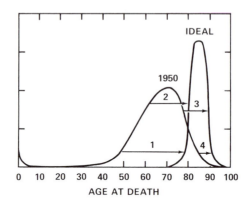

FIGURE 7-4.
The shift in life expectancy. Life expectancy increases at
all ages, but the increase becomes less with advancing
age.

20. Life expectancy from age 80 or 85 will increase also, although very much less.
Life expectancy above age 90 will remain nearly constant but also will increase
slightly. The decline in cardiovascular deaths in the last few years is already
having these effects, as shown in Table 7-2.

There is another way of looking at this critical phenomenon. At the turn of the
century, death occurred at an average age of 47 after an illness of only a few days.
Less than 1% of the average life span was spent in terminal illness. Gradually,
this figure has increased, with the emergence of chronic disease, so that a terminal illness taking up 10% or more of a life span is not unusual. With the
compression of infirmity, this fraction will again begin to decline.

Calculations of the financial effects of the compression of infirmity have been
made by the Futures Group of the National Science Foundation (Gordon, 1979).
In their study of life-extending technologies, this group emphasized rather fan-
ciful scenarios in which the life span itself was increased. However, they note in
passing the impact of "curve-squaring" technologies on the costs of health care,
with a remarkable prophecy. "Curve-squaring would *lower,* strikingly, per capita
costs for older persons, starting with the 45 to 49 age cohort. Chronic costs
would be delayed, and their duration reduced. In effect, they would tend to be
merged with the terminal costs; therefore, costs in the last few years of life would
be higher, but the overall cost per person would be reduced. Individuals would

TABLE 7-2.
Increases in Average Life Expectancy (years)

From Age	1910	1970 to 1977
70	3.1	0.9
75	2.6	0.8
80	2.1	0.8
85	1.8	0.6

Source: Data from the same sources cited for Table 3-1.

tend to stay healthy longer and decline more abruptly." The projected *decline* in health care costs is as much as 20%. These projections, similar to ours, are among the only suggestions ever made of the possibility of *reducing* health care expenditures in the future.

The rise of chronic disease, if successfully combatted, will be followed by the decline of these same diseases. The success story of combatting the acute illnesses can be followed, with a different script, by a success story of combatting the chronic universal illnesses, and the society with neither acute nor chronic disease will be a fascinating one.

First of November,—the Earthquake-day,—
There are traces of age in the one-hoss shay,
A general flavor of mild decay,
But nothing local, as one may say.
There couldn't be,—for the Deacon's art
Had made it so like in every part
That there wasn't a chance for one to start.

CHAPTER EIGHT

NATURAL LIFE
AND
NATURAL DEATH

wherein it is indicated that the diseases of aging
may be postponed by personal decisions

The concepts of natural life and natural
death emerge directly from our preceding discussions. Improvement in life
expectancy over the past century has resulted in a rectangularization of the
survival curve and a rising prevalence of chronic diseases with onset later in life.
The steepening downslope of the survival curve has begun to approach the ideal
curve that would be seen if there were no disease. There is ample reason to
believe that the chronic diseases may be slowed in their development, with a
consequent radical change in the health characteristics of the society. More and
more people will live into their 70's, 80's, and 90's free from premature illness;
more persons will realize a natural life. This once-utopian dream represents a
realistic projection based on solidly documented past trends and the optimistic,
but generally accepted, assumption that delay or prevention of the major chronic
afflictions is possible. There is certainly no reason to believe that new, as yet
unrecognized disorders will arise to take the place of the postponed diseases.

Natural life is not life without old age or senescence; it is life where debility occurs over a brief time period in the final phase of the rectangular curve. Disease and disability occur at this point because of markedly diminished organ reserve. In this chapter, we will explore the definitions of natural death and natural life as an introduction to our final chapters on human plasticity, personal choice, and social change.

NATURAL DEATH

Natural death is the inevitable outcome of linear decline of function in vital organ systems. At some point, declining organ function must become insufficient to sustain life. Even before this, restoration of homeostasis becomes impossible after ever-smaller internal or external environmental challenges. Eventually, in the final stage of senescence, natural death ensues. Totally natural death—death without any challenge whatsoever—is of course a conceptual ideal rarely realized, since perturbations, however trivial, are constantly occurring. Figure 8-1 illustrates the different points at which death may occur with the same linear decline in vitality. As vitality declines, the probability of succumbing increases dramatically, until a stage is reached where even minor disturbances are lethal. The attack of pneumonia, influenza, or appendicitis that would have been only an inconvenience in youth becomes a major life threat. With most acute infectious illnesses now under control, small environmental challenges to individual health are much more frequent than large ones. Presumably, the element of chance determines at what point one encounters the final challenge. At the very end of life, it becomes impossible to prevent death from even the smallest challenges. This is the stage of natural death, where even small deviations from equilibrium are irreversible.

The concept of premature death is distinctly different from the concept of natural death. Premature death results from a large, devastating challenge that cannot be overcome by the body's defenses, even though organ reserve and medical care may be adequate for smaller challenges. Accidents, overwhelming infections, metastatic cancer, and cardiovascular disease can all terminate life prematurely. In contrast, natural death can result from any of the frequent minor challenges as well as from the infrequent large challenges. Surviving a major challenge that almost causes premature death leaves one well again; in the final stages of natural senescence, no recovery is possible.

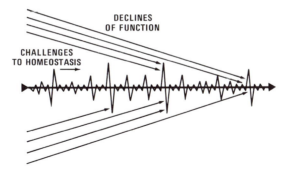

FIGURE 8-1.
Natural and premature death in a world of random
challenges. Death occurs when the magnitude of a
random environmental challenge exceeds the capacity
of an individual to restore homeostasis.

The two concepts, natural and premature death, exist on a continuum, and the
question of what is a small challenge and what is a large challenge becomes a
semantic one. Because of the brevity of the period of final senescence, the
question is usually resolved fairly quickly by time. With treatment, the person
with organ reserve may recover, whereas the person without organ reserve can
not.

The following examples may help to clarify the concept of natural death:

A man, age 87, lives in a small condominium near the beach with his wife. His
friends notice one day that he is "failing"; the doctor finds nothing wrong. For the
next three months he is "just not himself." One night he dies in his sleep. Such
scenarios are common in senior-citizen communities but are rarely either seen or
appreciated at medical facilities.

A woman, age 84, is in good health despite appearing increasingly frail. An
influenza epidemic spreads through the town. The woman develops influenza,
then bacterial bronchopneumonia, and dies in four days. This scenario is so common that influenza epidemics temporarily affect national death rates.

An 82-year-old man has problems of dizziness and heart failure resulting from
loss of cardiac reserve. Despite sequential medical use of digitalis, diuretics, pace-
makers, and oxygen, he is hospitalized ten times over a period of 18 months, with
the hospitalizations occurring at shorter intervals and being almost continuous
over the last three months before his death. This sequence is one where loss of
organ reserve in a particular organ, here the heart, becomes progressively limiting
and then relatively quickly fatal.

An 88-year-old woman with an infection of the bladder is admitted to the hospital
from a nursing home. When given intravenous fluids, she develops heart failure,
and the diuretics given to remove the fluid of the heart failure result in deterioration

of the kidney function. She is transferred to the intensive care unit, where oxygen is given and her every system is monitored with great care. She begins to bleed slightly from a stress ulcer in the stomach, and, during passage of a stomach tube to remove the blood, she vomits. A small amount of vomitus enters the lung, where an aspiration pneumonia develops. Despite oxygen treatment, she becomes comatose. A tracheotomy is performed, and a respirator is used to assist her breathing. Several other adverse events occur, the family is eventually told that there is no hope, and she dies in her seventh week in the hospital. This scenario is familiar to every physician—a trivial initial challenge in an individual without organ reserve leads to a sequence of catastrophes despite extraordinary care and despite extraordinary expenditure of resources. The medical care helps the patient to survive one catastrophe, or even several, but there is always another catastrophe awaiting its turn.

Natural death, defined generously as in these examples, is already common. Estimates are arbitrary, but both our personal clinical experience and inspection of the survival curves shown earlier suggest that perhaps one-third of all deaths now occur in the final stages of senescence—a natural death. Only a few years ago, few individuals survived the acute challenges to experience a natural death.

NATURAL LIFE

Human lifestyles today are certainly different from those of our remote ancestors. Over hundreds of thousands of years, the progress of civilization has substantially diminished the problems of immediate survival; nevertheless, it has substituted new problems of its own. Our fad diets, refined foods with additives, time stresses, cigarettes, paucity of exercise, polluted air and water, drug ingestions, and complex modern lifestyles were unknown to our hunter–gatherer ancestors. We live longer on the average than our ancestors because of our ability to control acute diseases. We are now in a position to combat the chronic diseases that are presently responsible for the vast majority of premature deaths. These chronic diseases appear, for the most part, to result from unnatural lifestyles. We define *unnatural* in this sense to mean a relatively recent practice for which there has as yet been no opportunity for evolutionary response by natural selection.

A central thesis of this book is that our lives can be freed of disease as chronic diseases are postponed. Lifestyle changes are required for postponement of these diseases. The natural aging process then becomes the major factor limiting our life span; senescence rather than disease will control our potential destiny.

What reversible factors are presently associated with loss of organ reserve? Senescence and aging, as well as disease, are affected by the risk factors that predispose to chronic illness. Here we review the relationship of alcohol abuse, cigarette smoking, diet, and exercise to health and to natural aging.

Alcohol Abuse

Aside from the morbidity and personal tragedies resulting from alcoholic intoxication, alcohol makes a major contribution to premature death through automobile and other accidents. These deaths involve not only drunk drivers but also family members and innocent bystanders of all ages; these deaths now represent the fourth largest cause of years of life lost in the United States. A second contribution of alcohol to premature death results from alcoholic liver disease—cirrhosis, hepatitis, and rapidly fatal liver cancer. In addition, alcoholism is associated with dementia, homicide, and suicide. There is no doubt that excessive alcohol consumption is a major health hazard associated with increased premature mortality. In the next chapter, we examine the findings that depression, lack of coping skills, and decline in self-image from alcoholism contribute also to rapid aging.

Cigarette Smoking

Cigarette smoking is the most important cause of three major chronic diseases—lung cancer, emphysema, and cardiovascular disease. Malignant neoplasms are the second leading cause of death in the United States today. Thirty percent of these deaths result from lung cancer, and ninety percent of the lung cancers are caused by cigarette smoking. The more cigarettes smoked, the higher is the probability of developing lung cancer. Ten years after smoking is stopped, the risk of lung cancer returns to the level of the nonsmoker. Essentially all cases of emphysema and chronic bronchitis result from cigarette smoking. Emphysema and bronchitis together are the eleventh leading cause of death in the United States. Atherosclerosis, with its consequent heart disease and stroke, is the most frequent cause of death in the United States by a wide margin. Cigarette smoking is one of the three major risk factors for the development of atherosclerosis; the other two are hypertension and elevated serum low-density cholesterol, also both potentially controllable. There is no doubt that elimination of cigarette smoking would be a major contribution to the elimination of premature death.

Diet

Speculation about the malevolent contributions of diet to premature morbidity and mortality is hazardous. Although dietary theories are in abundance, conclusive evidence to support the frequently made recommendations is meager. The major dietary problem in Western industrialized societies today is overeating, resulting in obesity. In 1959, the experience of U.S. life insurance companies from 1935 to 1954 was reported as the Build and Blood Pressure Study (BBPS), and tables of desirable weights by height were prepared by the Metropolitan Life Insurance Company. The study demonstrated that increased weight is associated with an increased risk of mortality. Minimum mortality risk occurred for lean persons whose weights were well below the average weight for height. These weight tables based on the BBPS have since served as the standard reference for ideal weight. Recently reported results of the Framingham study are not fully in accord with these insurance company conclusions. In the Framingham study, very lean subjects have as great a mortality risk as obese subjects. We are left with considerable uncertainty as to what ideal weight actually is. However, it is clear that persons with extreme obesity have an increased mortality risk and that obese subjects with certain conditions, such as hypertension, diabetes mellitus, and elevated blood lipids, can achieve improvement in these conditions by weight loss.

Are there dietary strategies other than avoiding extreme obesity that will improve life expectancy or life quality? Does a low cholesterol, low saturated fat, high fiber, low salt diet decrease morbidity and mortality in the general population? Here again there is considerable controversy, and no definitive studies have been performed. Persons less than 50 years old with elevated total serum cholesterol levels definitely have an increased risk of atherosclerotic disease as compared with persons of the same age with normal cholesterol levels. These associations are more complicated when the cholesterol-carrying particles in the blood are analyzed in detail. Most of the cholesterol in the blood is carried in the particle called low density lipoprotein (LDL), and about 25% of the cholesterol is carried in high density lipoprotein (HDL). Persons with elevated LDL cholesterol levels have an increased risk of cardiovascular disease at all ages; persons with elevated HDL cholesterol levels have a decreased risk. Thus, strategies that lower serum LDL cholesterol, such as low cholesterol diets, low saturated fat diets, and weight reduction, would be expected to decrease the risk of premature atherosclerosis. A similar benefit would be expected from increases in serum HDL cholesterol, such as occurs with exercise.

In animal studies, including nonhuman primates, experimentally elevated serum LDL cholesterol levels lead to severe atherosclerosis, which can be reversed by lowering these levels back to normal. In humans, it remains to be conclusively demonstrated that lowering LDL cholesterol levels or raising HDL cholesterol levels can reverse or prevent the formation of atherosclerotic plaques and can result in a subsequent reduction in cardiovascular mortality. Still, native Japanese, with vastly different diet and very much lower serum cholesterol levels, have essentially no atherosclerosis. Some Japanese, who emigrate to this country and experience dietary and other changes, develop the disease. "Natural" diets—avoiding refined carbohydrates and including high fiber—have been associated by some with decreased cancer of the colon, diverticulitis, and hemorrhoids. In addition, refined sugars have been implicated by some as a contributing cause of dental caries. Some have maintained that overeating in the first two years of life increases the number of fat cells and thus represents a cause of adult obesity. We counsel moderation with any of the potentially adverse dietary components, and believe, until the evidence is in, that a moderately low salt, low animal fat, high fiber, low refined carbohydrate diet is indicated for most persons.

Exercise

What is the role of exercise in the elimination of premature cardiovascular disease and mortality? Animal studies have convincingly demonstrated that exercise can delay the development of atherosclerosis. For example, Kramsch and coworkers studied sedentary and treadmill-exercised monkeys over a two-year period. Sedentary monkeys on a high cholesterol diet showed marked atherosclerotic narrowing of the coronary arteries by electrocardiograms, angiography, and postmortem exams; exercised monkeys on the same high cholesterol diet showed significantly less atherosclerosis. In humans, for obvious reasons, no such studies are possible; the evidence is weaker but still strongly suggestive.

Data from the Framingham study show a correlation between decreased physical activity level and cardiovascular mortality and between decreased physical activity and the major risk factors of hypertension, elevated serum cholesterol, and cigarette smoking. Studies by Paffenbarger of longshoremen and of college alumni suggest that decreased physical activity, cigarette smoking, and hypertension each independently increases the risk of heart attacks. No definitive evidence from a randomized study will ever be available, since such studies are both impractical and do not meet present ethical guidelines. However, there are good reasons to expect that such studies would be positive. Numerous studies convincingly show that exercise in the form of walking, jogging, skiing, or marathon running increases serum HDL cholesterol. Good studies have also shown that exercise leads to improvement in glucose tolerance, independent of weight loss, in diabetics and nondiabetics. To the extent that exercise increases collateral circulation to the heart and decreases obesity (with a consequent lowering of blood pressure, blood sugar, and blood lipids), benefits would be expected. In evolutionary terms, exercise is highly natural, since our culture's relative inactivity has only been possible since the onset of the industrial revolution.

LIFESTYLES AND HEART DISEASE

High blood pressure is one of the major risks for premature morbidity and mortality from cardiovascular disease. Two important studies have demonstrated beyond doubt that treatment of hypertension is beneficial. In the 1960s, the VA Cooperative Study showed that treatment of moderate and severe hypertension reduced morbidity from cardiovascular disease. Recently, the Hypertension Detection and Follow-Up Program convincingly demonstrated that treatment of all degrees of hypertension, including mild hypertension, significantly reduces cardiovascular mortality. These two exciting studies form the groundwork for an aggressive approach to treatment. There is every reason to expect such an approach to help reduce premature cardiovascular disease. Interestingly, natural approaches to blood pressure control, such as weight loss, salt restriction, and stress reduction, are now being used more and more. They appear to be effective at times in reducing blood pressure and in decreasing the need for medication.

Recently, there has been a dramatic decline of mortality due to ischemic heart disease (heart attacks resulting from atherosclerosis of the coronary arteries). During the eight-year period between 1968 and 1976 in the United States, there was an overall decline in ischemic heart disease mortality of 20.7%. As shown in Table 8-1, this decline occurred in all age groups and for both males and females. The percentage decline was greatest in the age range between 25 and 45 years; females showed a greater percentage decline than males in all age ranges. A similar decline has been observed in Canada, Australia, and Finland, but not in England and Wales.

The reasons for this striking decrease in mortality from coronary heart disease remain speculative. Has it resulted from a reduction in cardiovascular risk factors with increased exercise, better diets, less cigarette smoking, and more effective treatment of hypertension? Has it resulted from improved medical care delivery

TABLE 8-1.
Percentage Decline in Ischemic Heart Disease Mortality in the United States,
1968–1976

Age (years)	Both Sexes	Males	Females
25–34	31.3	26.0	42.4
35–44	28.9	27.3	35.7
45–54	21.3	21.1	22.0
55–64	21.0	20.4	22.1
65–74	23.1	20.2	26.8
75–84	16.1	12.8	17.3
85 and over	20.8	18.5	21.6

with coronary care units, early detection, rapid response of emergency services
in the field, coronary-artery bypass surgery, and improved medical treatment of
ischemic heart disease? Has there been a decreased incidence of ischemic heart
disease or a better delivery of medical services or both? Probably each of these
factors has contributed to some extent.

The attainment of natural life is increasingly linked to personal behavior.
Choices about diet, exercise, cigarette smoking, alcohol consumption, and drug
compliance for hypertension are already firmly associated with health outcomes.
The leading lethal diseases of the past have been effectively combatted and are
now being replaced by universal, chronic conditions which are not easily treated.
Yet, much of the current health care system is focused on the diagnosis and
treatment of these chronic diseases at the symptomatic stage, too late to affect
outcomes decisively. In the prophetic view of McKeown (pp. xv–xvi), "Medical
science and services are misdirected, and society's investment in health is not
well used, because they rest on an erroneous assumption about the basis of
human health. It is assumed that the body can be regarded as a machine whose
protection from disease and its effects depends primarily on internal intervention. The approach has led to indifference to the external influences and personal
behavior which are the predominant determinants of health."

The era of natural life and natural death lies ahead; its attainment will require
a fundamental shift in personal and societal priorities. The concepts interrelate
and interplay. Control of acute disease prevents premature death and allows the
occasional occurrence of natural death. Postponement of chronic diseases in
part requires natural lifestyles. Affirmation of natural lifestyles increases the likelihood of natural life followed by natural death.

For the wheels were just as strong as the thills,
And the floor was just as strong as the sills,
And the panels just as strong as the floor,
And the whipple-tree neither less nor more,
And the back crossbar as strong as the fore,
And spring and axle and hub *encore.*
And yet, *as a whole,* it is past a doubt
In another hour it will be *worn out!*

CHAPTER NINE

THE PLASTICITY
OF AGING

wherein the major manifestations of senescence
are shown to be modifiable

If we must die, at a time common to our
species and varied only by the nature of a normal biological distribution, can we
not at least avoid aging until the last possible moment? Can we, in a limited sense
at least, find ways to preserve our youth and vigor? Can aging be delayed? To
what extent are the phenomena of aging thus plastic and modifiable?

The very words *aging* and *senescence* complicate our consideration of these
questions because we cannot state very clearly what they mean. However, we can
say that aging and senescence are only loosely related to increasing chronological
age. Persons of the same chronological age often have very different physiological
or mental ages. Many older individuals are youthful with regard to certain attributes and aged with regard to others. We cannot speak accurately of *aging* as a
general term; rather, we must specify the particular attribute of aging that we
wish to consider.

This problem is acutely evident if we review the search for the perfect marker
of aging. Investigators have studied literally scores of possible markers. These

include anatomical changes, such as the graying of hair, the loss of skin elasticity, the development of opacities in the ocular lens, and the increase in rigidity of the large arteries. Possible markers include physiological variables, such as cardiac reserve, measures of kidney clearance of waste materials, lung vital capacity or maximal breathing rate, liver detoxification of drugs, reaction time, and nerve conduction velocities. Other markers include psychological variables, such as short-term memory, crystallized and fluid intelligence, and social interaction.

Two principal observations result from these many studies. First, none of the proposed variables is a satisfactory marker of aging. None of them correlates very well with the others; none correlates very well with chronological age; and none correlates very well with indexes constructed from a number of observations (Table 9-1). To emphasize this poor performance, note that the best correlations come from such variables as the hair graying score (percentage of gray hairs in the armpits) and skin elasticity (usually measured by the time it takes for a pinch of skin to return to its original position after being released). The failure of graying of hair to correlate consistently with aging is a matter of daily observation, as is the observation of chronologically very youthful persons with very old-appearing skin.

Second, almost everything declines with age. For practically every variable measured in large groups of people, the average value is highest in the decade from age 20 to age 30, then slowly declines at a practically constant rate over the subsequent years. This linear decline as a function of chronological age has been described in Chapter Three. Here we are concerned more with what this observation hides than with what it reveals.

VARIABILITY

Variability is the critical dimension overlooked when only the average results of large groups are considered. Very few individuals are fairly represented by these average values; instead, most individuals are represented in the "scatter" around the average. And this scatter or variability behaves in a fascinating way with increasing age—it increases. Usually, we expect that a measurement will show its greatest variability at the highest performance levels; this would represent a world in which individuals were most different at the age of 20 to 30 and became more alike as their powers declined with advancing years. The very opposite is true. Differences between individuals, usually represented statistically by the

TABLE 9-1.
Some Proposed Marker Variables for Aging

Test	Correlation with Age
Hair graying score	0.72
Skin elasticity	0.60
Audiometry	0.59
Vibrometer	0.54
Systolic blood pressure	0.52
Light extinction test	0.49
Reaction time, ruler test	0.48
Flicker-fusion frequency	−0.48
Visual acuity	−0.43
Diastolic blood pressure	0.41
Total vital capacity	−0.40
Hand grip strength	−0.32
Heart size	0.29
Serum cholesterol	0.23
One-second expiratory volume	−0.13

Source: After A. Comfort, *The Biology of Senescence,* Third Edition, Elsevier, 1979.

standard deviation from the mean, increase with advancing calendar age. By any standard of aging we choose to use, we age at different rates, and the differences between us grow greater as we grow older! The different rates again prove, in one sense, that chronological age itself is not a good marker for aging. In a more profound sense, however, increasing variation with age suggests that there must be a reason for the differences. If we could understand the reasons, we might be able to exchange a rapid rate of aging for a slower one—we might be able to postpone the aging process.

A second neglected area has been the long-term study of aging. Practically all work has been cross-sectional in nature, with the investigator making observations of persons of different ages at the same time. This is the easiest and least expensive way to make observations, but it obscures two major problems. First, persons of differing ages have had different cultural experiences, resulting in differences between generations in such areas as sexual conduct, experiences of wars and famines, exposure to various toxins, and level of physical activity. From a cross-sectional study, we cannot exclude the possibility that some of the observed decline in function with age is a result of such generational (cohort) effects. These cohort effects include not only the experience of major historical events but also changes in the social environment, such as long-term trends in sanitation, standard of living, nutrition, industrialization, and the spread of sedentary occupations.

Second, in cross-sectional studies, we cannot track the route by which an individual reaches the observed level of performance. Was it a regular progression or an irregular one? Was the progression slow and then steep or steep and then slow? So, for most studies, we have only a very partial view of the progression of the individual through time and of the effect of the social setting on the measurement of aging.

Even with the few longitudinal studies, such as those at Duke, Berkeley, and Baltimore, we are left with alternative explanations for the observations. These studies are only a few years old, so they do not answer questions about the impact of the Great Depression or World War I or II. Even more importantly, they are still confounded by expected societal roles for persons of different ages. For example, physical activity and many of the physiological variables associated with activity decline in later life. The worker becomes foreman and then manager. Active participation in sports is more limited and then discontinued. The retired person has been expected to "take it easy" as the reward for a life of hard work. Could the decline in activity be responsible for the decline in the aging variables? Even these few good studies have not adequately addressed questions of individual variation, and none has yet attempted to track individual lifelines over time.

These concerns may seem unnecessarily technical, but they leave us with the suspicion that the most important aspects of human aging have been bypassed as research topics. We offer this suspicion as a prediction. We predict that some markers of aging cannot be changed by any reasonable intervention, and these represent the inexorable changes of increasing age. We predict, however, that many other markers can be readily modified, and the process of aging with regard to these variables can be slowed or stopped. To make our prediction more specific, we predict that the graying of hair, the elasticity of skin, the rigidity of the arteries, the kidney function, and the opacification of the lens of the eye cannot be changed. And we predict that exercise tolerance, maximal breathing rate, cardiac reserve, reaction time, physical strength, short-term memory, intelligence as measured by intelligence tests, ambulatory abilities, and social abilities can be maintained or even improved with advancing age.

Because aging is not one thing but many, approaches to modification of aging must focus on the particular attribute to be changed. We may anticipate success in some instances and lack of success in others. Given our present knowledge, we cannot be certain of all the areas where improvement is impossible. We do already know, however, of some areas where improvement with increasing age is readily accomplishable. Happily, this list is quite impressive. It shows that we can improve physical function, mental function, and social function within very broad biological limits. These are the capacities about which we worry the most as we grow older, and they fortunately manifest the plasticity of aging. Long before the term *plastic* was linked to particular chemical polymers, it had a more general meaning encompassing the possibility of remolding and of change. Behavioral scientists find the term apt for description of aging phenomena.

PLASTICITY

The concept of plasticity builds on the observation of variability. It means that the future capability for a given attribute is not fixed, predestined, and inevitable, but may be modified. It implies that either improvement or regression in function may occur over time. Our concern here is with improvement, and positive changes may occur with any combination of three factors: (1) the elimination of the variability caused by disease, (2) taking advantage of favorable changes accruing to an entire age group (cohort), or (3) improvement with time in the individual. This last possibility, swimming against the stream, is effected by use of the desired faculty, and it applies equally well to physical, mental, or social markers of aging.

PLASTICITY BY DECREASE IN UNIVERSAL, CHRONIC DISEASE

As a population ages, an increasing proportion of the population suffers from illness. In our time, as we have noted, the vast majority of illness is universal, progressive, and chronic. Before such diseases are fatal, they cause months or years of decreasing function, pain, and associated functional decrements due to depression, decreased socialization, and diminished function as a result of medications.

Part of the increased variability of increased age is due simply to the inclusion of a larger proportion of ill persons in the population. If we eliminate the sick people, the average function of the entire group gets better, and the variability declines slightly. With a successful strategy to postpone chronic illness, as out-lined in the previous chapters, the number of physically infirm people will decrease as the increasing age at onset of illness compresses the span of chronic illness against the finite species life span.

Much of what we associate with aging is actually chronic illness. The breath-lessness of emphysema, activity-limiting heart pain or intermittent leg pains while walking, the fatigue of congestive heart failure, the blindness or neuropathy of diabetes, and the knee pain of osteoarthritis are all intuitively associated with aging. If the onset of these conditions is postponed, then we as a population will achieve a degree of preservation of youth and vigor. And the strategies for control of chronic disease are, as noted previously, in large part individual ones. The individual must exercise personal choice and personal discipline in lifestyle. Plasticity with regard to the onset of first chronic medical infirmity has been clearly documented in a number of instances, but the appropriate decisions and actions must be undertaken by the individual.

It is difficult to exclude all ill persons from a study of elderly populations, since chronic illnesses progress for a long time below the clinical threshold and may cause decrements in performance before they can be diagnosed. But insofar as possible, such individuals have been excluded from most of the major lon-gitudinal studies. And, after such exclusion, most of the variability among indi-viduals persists. For further improvement, we may look to the society, to factors affecting an entire cohort.

PLASTICITY BY COHORT CHANGES

As the years pass, each generation experiences its own unique set of conditioning influences, which affect its perspective on present events, its lifestyle choices, its reaction patterns, and ultimately its health. Health is influenced, certainly, by such events as wars, famines, plagues, fires, floods, and earthquakes. Health is also influenced by the automobile, the telephone, economic depressions, free-ways, traffic jams, pollution, and television. A cohort is simply a group of people born at the same time, who thus share the same historical and social milieu as they age.

Among the most influential observations on the plasticity of cohort aging are those of Nesselroade, Schaie, and Baltes, who carefully studied the psychological functioning of a group of individuals in 1956 and then meticulously restudied the same group with the same tests in 1963. The results of this well-known and controversial study are typified in the data of Figure 9-1. Not surprisingly, when subjects were grouped by age, performance declined with advancing age, both in 1956 and in 1963. Indeed, the solid lines in Figure 9-1 are typical for almost any aging marker studied by an investigator; in this case, the marker was intelligence, using well-validated tests for crystallized, factual intelligence. Note the maximal performance plateau in the third decade and the almost linear decline thereafter.

However, the dashed lines of Figure 9-1 indicate the more exciting observation—all age groups improved their performance over this seven-year period. In fact, the older groups improved more than the younger ones. Individuals aged 77 scored better on this intelligence test than they had at age 70. If these study subjects were representative of the nation as a whole, and they probably were, then the entire nation got "smarter" over a seven-year period. Cross-sectional studies missed this striking finding, which demonstrates that entire groups of individuals can increase their intelligence test scores with age under certain circumstances.

The explanation for this phenomenon is not certain. It may be related to the development of television. During this period, television entered nearly every home in the United States, bringing commentators with larger vocabularies into

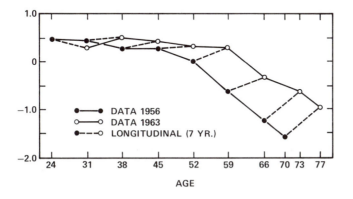

FIGURE 9-1.
Improvement of crystallized intelligence in selected study groups in the United States over a seven-year period.
(Redrawn with permission from J. Nesselroade, K. Schaie, and P. B. Baltes, *Journal of Gerontology* 1972, 27:222–228.)

the living room. World events were brought closer, cultural events could now be viewed even in rural areas, and the television quiz shows that were popular then involved recall and use of specific factual material; these programs were emulated in many family games. Perhaps it is not surprising that older individuals long out of school were the major beneficiaries of the new information network provided by television.

Of course, what goes up often comes down. All time periods are not so favorable, and the national intelligence may have made a number of unobserved shifts, since studies of this kind are unusual. For example, the college entrance examination scores in the United States are currently in a steady fifteen-year decline, indicating that, as measured by a standardized test administered to large numbers of persons, the nation now is becoming on the average less knowledgeable. As compared with previous cohorts, vocabularies are declining, factual knowledge is decreasing, and familiarity with numerical concepts is decreasing. Quite possibly, this phenomenon extends through all cohorts, and quite possibly, it is again due to television, this time to the large number of hours the average individual spends viewing material seemingly selected for its banal content.

But the observation that traditional markers of aging can improve for entire populations is most heartening. If populations of various ages can improve, then an individual must certainly be able to improve. Senescence in certain markers of aging is not inevitable. We can get better, not just older. Such cohort studies have provided the stimulus for the study of aging modification in the individual, which we call individual plasticity.

INDIVIDUAL PLASTICITY

Physical Plasticity

Many aging markers can be rather easily modified by the individual. This statement is not as surprising as it might first appear, since it really only says that our capacity for self-improvement continues with minimal impairment into late adult life. For illustration, consider the vigorous activity of marathon running. Figure 9-2 shows the world record marathon performance in men from age 10 to age 79 by year of age. Note how closely this curve of maximal human performance follows the pattern of other markers of aging. Performance is maximal from age 20 to age 30, then declines linearly for many years.

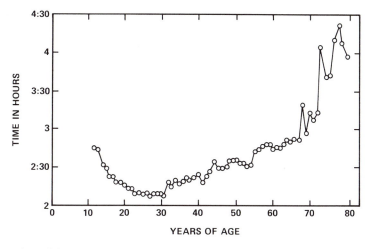

FIGURE 9-2.
World record marathon times for men, ages 10 to 79. (Data from
Runner's World, 1980.)

Senescence in marathon running occurs at an average rate of about two minutes per year. But consider instead the individual variability at each age. Within
the same age group, say, at age 40, the time required for a healthy individual to
traverse 26 miles on foot varies from 2 hours and 30 minutes to two days or
more. The variability due to age is very much less than the variability due to
other factors. Chronological age is not a very important predictor of performance
in marathon running. A respectable marathon time of 3½ hours in middle life
is not a world record unless the individual is over 70 years old. (A 65-year-old
man recently has beaten the 1908 world record.) The important predictor of
marathon performance is practice.

The recent renaissance in human running proves the plasticity of this aging
marker in our daily encounters. The little old lady in tennis shoes is now running
5 miles a day in carefully designed jogging footwear. Performance improvements
accrue to everyone who works at it. Indeed, performance is linked, in many
training programs, to the number of miles per week that are run. This jogging
example is a clear one because the causal factors are so obvious and because
the phenomenon has been quite well studied. Joggers lose weight, decrease
their blood pressure, increase their vital capacity, decrease their serum cholesterol, increase their high density lipoproteins, improve their maximum breathing
capacity, and improve their cardiac reserve. Thus, by a single maneuver, the
runner has proved individual plasticity for a large number of the proposed aging
markers listed in Table 9-1. And this plasticity can be demonstrated at any age.

Moreover, the mechanism necessary to achieve plasticity in physical activity is self-evident. You have to use the faculty. You have to jog to improve your personal record times. You have to work at it, use self-discipline, make personal decisions. You have to practice. You may choose to improve your performance, or you may choose not to, but if you really want to change these markers of aging, they can be changed. Individual plasticity is clearly possible.

Physical plasticity extends far beyond increasing cardiovascular reserve. Spirduso has studied reaction times in individuals of different ages. Individuals ages 50 to 70 who played racquet sports, entailing quick reactions, had reaction times similar to sedentary individuals aged 20 to 30. In a second study, older runners were found to have maintained the same quick reactions. Even nerve conduction velocity, once felt to be linked immutably to age, appears to be only inconsistently related to years of life and may possibly improve with activity.

Plasticity of Intellectual Aging

Physical fitness as an example of plasticity is perhaps too obvious, since few people would care to argue that physical performance could not usually be improved. What about plasticity in mental function? What about intelligence? Is there not an inexorable downward trend with regard to the IQ? Surely this marker of aging, as measured by tests designed to detect capability rather than factual knowledge, cannot be altered. Intelligence, it seems, must decline with age.

But we saw previously that crystallized intelligence can improve in an entire cohort, implying that it must be improvable in an individual. Plemons and coworkers designed an ingenious experiment to examine the degree to which fluid intelligence (cognitive flexibility) could be modified in aged subjects. They studied 30 subjects, mostly female, ages 59 to 85 years (average, 70 years). After dividing the subjects into two comparable groups on the basis of a pretest of IQ, they gave eight hours of training in figural relations (over four weeks) to one group, and then they retested both groups several times.

Figural relations is a major component of cognitive flexibility or fluid intelligence as presently conceived. This capacity can be measured by a standard diagnostic test closely related to course content or by a somewhat different test devised by Cattell and Horn. Other aspects of IQ testing can be classed as distantly related (inductive reasoning) or very distantly related (verbal comprehension).

Plemons and coworkers found the results shown in Figure 9-3. The group that had been trained markedly increased their scores on this aspect of the IQ test; the control group did not. In subsequent retesting, the improved scores were

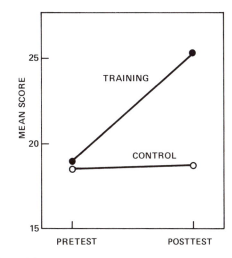

FIGURE 9-3.
Improvement of fluid intelligence in two groups
(average age, 70 years). (Redrawn with permission
from J. K. Plemons, S. L. Willis, and P. B. Baltes, *Journal
of Gerontology* 1978, 33:224–231.)

maintained for at least four months, although the control group also improved
as they became more familiar with the test materials. The differences were significant statistically, and they clearly show that IQ test performance is plastic,
even in the eighth decade.

These trained subjects also improved performance on the closely related Cattell–Horn Figural Relations Tests, but there was no change in scores for induction
or for verbal comprehension. If the test was not closely related to the training,
no effect could be determined. Thus, plasticity in intelligence is quite specific to
the subject matter presented in the training program. The specific faculty must
be exercised for it to be improved.

Plasticity of Memory

Perhaps, then, we can accept that older persons are able to improve IQ test
performance. But surely such subjects could not improve their memories. Everyone knows that you get forgetful as you get older. There are problems in storing
the short-term memories in the brain, or in finding them and getting them out
again. These problems must be biologically determined and unmodifiable.

However, Langer and coworkers have examined these propositions and have found, again, the opposite of the conventional wisdom. These investigators studied nursing home residents averaging 80 years of age. They performed two experiments using good scientific design, including blinded observers, objective tests, and matched assignment to study or control groups. First, they looked at memory effects from interviews, during which young interviewers engaged the subjects in mutual self-disclosure, forcing them in effect to think about and consider new topics. In the second experiment, the interviewers rewarded the subjects with prizes for being able to remember certain recent events. Nurses who were unaware of the study rated the patients carefully, and several standard memory tests were given.

The results were striking. Residents who were made to interact and those who were rewarded for correct memories showed memory improvement relative to those to whom the same amount of attention was given without the same rewards or interactions. Moreover, nurses reported greater sociability, greater self-initiating behavior, improved awareness, increased activity, and even better health in the treated groups. A number of other studies have shown that older persons benefit particularly from training in the use of "retrieval cues." Short-term memory, usually thought to be a marker of aging, is plastic. It can be improved.

The parallels among plasticity of memory, intelligence, and physical fitness should be evident. Use of a faculty is associated with improvement of that faculty. One final example, social interaction, will emphasize this association.

Plasticity of Social Interaction

Social isolation frequently accompanies old age. A number of studies have shown increased death rates for the institutionalized aged, particularly in the first few weeks of nursing home residence. Adverse health events have seemed to increase for persons who are lonely, isolated, unhappy, and separated from family and friends.

Langer and coworkers performed a series of experiments to determine the effect, if any, of increasing personal choice and personal responsibility for nursing home residents. Experimental subjects, averaging about 80 years of age, were told to treat the nursing home as their own and to make decisions just as they would at home. They were encouraged to select a house plant for their room and to take care of it. They could choose whether they wanted to see a movie, and when. They were told "it's your life, and you can make of it anything that you want." Surely this was the simplest and most modest intervention imaginable.

Control subjects were told the opposite. The staff was there to make them happy. If they needed anything, just ask. There were each given house plants and told that the staff would take care of them and water them. They were assigned to see movies at specific times.

Both groups were carefully assessed for the effects of induced responsibility, with spectacular results. The control group did not change, but the experimental group reported themselves happier and more active. Nurses rated them improved and participating in a much wider range of activities. After eighteen months, they were more vigorous, more socially active, and more self-initiating. Strikingly, after eighteen months, only 15% of the experimental group had died, whereas 30% of the control group had died.

These experiments are among the very few attempts to measure the effects of deliberate interventions on aspects of the aging process. Not only are the results very promising, they display a consistent theme of demonstrating the plasticity of aging by encouraging personal activity and personal choice. A number of theoretical considerations underlie such studies—for example, the concepts of learned helplessness, psychological defense mechanisms, and cognitive dissonance.

Learned helplessness has been proposed by Seligman and others to underlie many physical and psychological malfunctions. A wide range of animal and human observations support the general concept that the ability to make and execute one's own choices is critical to well-being. For example, wild rats suffer sudden death when forced to swim in a vat of water without possibility of escape; when provided hope of rescue, they can swim for days. Depression, premature illness, and death in humans can be linked to the same kinds of situations— hopeless and with no options. The theories of learned helplessness suggest that personal decision making is crucial to health.

Psychological health and physical health have been linked in a number of studies. Among the most impressive are the studies of Valliant and coworkers, who have carefully studied a group of college men for four decades. Many of those with poor psychological health died or became chronically ill prior to age 53 (18 of 48), whereas those with good psychological health did not (2 of 59). Moreover, good psychological health could be correlated with particular mechanisms of dealing with life problems and crises, among them altruism, humor, and suppression. These men thought positively, looked forward, stayed active, and stayed well. Paffenbarger, studying the same group of men, noted that physical activity as adults, not as students, was correlated with the best health (see reference for Chapter Eight).

In a related theory, Totman has emphasized the role of reduction in cognitive dissonance after personal decision making as a positive health force. After we make a decision, we adopt behaviors that justify that decision to ourselves and to others. The need to justify the decision (reduce dissonance) is greatest if the decision was a close one and could have gone either way. Much of the placebo effect may be related to making a difficult choice to use a controversial agent and then feeling the psychological necessity to fulfill the hopes entailed by the decision.

These theoretical constructions again suggest that health benefits may result from particular personal decisions. A wider literature discusses similar notions under the heading of "locus of control." Those individuals who control their own destiny do much better in a variety of situations then do those whose locus of control is external to them, who are controlled by others or by the environment.

We recognize some problems with the previous discussion. For those not familiar with the several disciplines involved, the descriptions are dry and somewhat ponderous. For those familiar with the work, they are selective, superficial, and a bit pejorative. Interested readers are referred to the original authors, who can speak for themselves better than we can for them. We do not intend to suggest that there is unanimous agreement with the concepts we have discussed or that the studies themselves are beyond controversy. Confirming studies have generally not yet been performed, and many of the present studies come from only two or three groups of investigators.

We do suggest that there is already evidence for substantial plasticity in aging with regard to many variables, including those of the greatest concern to all of us who worry from time to time about growing old. We further suggest that this evidence is compelling, growing, and coherent in theory. And we note the common theme from physicians, exercise physiologists, psychiatrists, and psychologists that control of the aging process is intimately connected with personal decisions and resulting actions and activities.

In fact, from one reference point, this whole set of questions reduces to common sense. If we accept the idea that aging is a set of separate processes, we recognize immediately that most of the processes can be modified; indeed, this is the principle behind all academic and physical education. The studies cited here only document that you can still learn and change when you are older, that old dogs indeed can learn new tricks. From this simple observation comes the more profound conclusion that many aspects of aging are under personal control.

Plasticity, like other phenomena, must have its ultimate genesis in events at the molecular or cellular level. Finch and others have reviewed the growing experimental evidence for such plasticity in animal experiments. Some aging changes in the rat hypothalamus, for example, can be altered by hormonal changes. Dietary manipulations also can lead to such changes. Finch has argued strongly that chronological time is only an associated variable for cellular aging and that the term *age-dependent* may well give way in part to *event-dependent* for many cellular phenomena. Cells can improve their function with time under some circumstances.

THE LIMITS OF PLASTICITY

If we return to the marathon runners of Figure 9-2, we must reaffirm that there is an age gradient, even if it is relatively small as compared with individual variation within an age group. If our middle-aged runner wishes to maintain the same elapsed time for the marathon over many years, the effort required in the training program must increase each year. For the same performance level, the time required for training will increase each year. The older runner becomes like Sisyphus, except that, with each trip up the hill, the stone becomes heavier. When we improve performance against the gradient, we can do so only because our previous performance did not use all of our potential. If we are performing at our limit, we cannot escape an age decrement, and we must instead take solace in the fact that the decrement is usually quite small from year to year.

If maintaining performance takes ever more time and effort as we age, then we are inevitably forced to another set of choices, since we will be increasingly unable to maintain function in all of the components of aging. We must choose where not to age. We must choose to strive for a somewhat improved level of ability in many areas or a much higher level in just a few areas.

Finally, there is the rectangular curve. Nothing goes on forever. At the end of the linear period of slow age decrement comes the period of abrupt decrement. Some psychologists have called this phenomenon the "terminal drop," describing the same events for cognitive function that we have described for lost reserve function of body organs. The goal of plasticity is to maintain function until the very end of the life span. The final limit to the plasticity of aging is the upper bound of the rectangular curve.

At half past nine by the meet'n'-house clock,—
Just the hour of the Earthquake shock!
What do you think the parson found,
When he got up and stared around?
The poor old chaise in a heap or mound,
As if it had been to the mill and ground!

CHAPTER TEN

TRIUMPH
AND
DESPAIR

wherein the burden of personal choice
is observed to present an existential conflict

The issues of human aging are squarely joined at the point of inescapable personal choice. In this chapter, we will explore the dilemmas presented by individual choices and their consequences.

Three central postulates of human aging emerge from our discussions in previous chapters. First, the life span is fixed. Data supporting this hypothesis have been presented from anthropology, from history, from contemporary observation, from evolutionary theory, from experimental observations on isolated cell populations, and from observed declines in organ function with age. There are no contrary data, and this postulate, representing the "bad news," is firmly established.

Second, many aspects of what we commonly think of as aging, perhaps most, are plastic and may be modified. This is the "good news," and it is supported by theoretical and experimental observations from physiology, medicine, psychology, sociology, and other disciplines. The postponement of manifestations of aging rectangularizes the vigor curve, always against the limit of a finite life span.

Third, the major requirement for the postponement of aging is exercise of the specific faculty. Such exercise requires personal choice and personal effort. The personal choices necessary to delay the onset of physical and mental aging phenomena include physical activity to delay declines in cardiopulmonary and musculoskeletal reserve, dietary and weight control to decrease diseases linked to these factors, habit moderation to minimize chances of the serious diseases caused by excessive cigarette smoking, alcohol ingestion, and drug usage, active mental problem-solving activity to enhance capabilities in these areas, and intensive social interaction to maintain skills and to provide stimulation necessary for continued individual growth.

The result of these postulates is shown schematically in Figure 10-1, where, for the first time, we plot curves for individuals in a rectangular form. Linear senescence is represented by the straight diagonal line. In fact, the extremely inactive life would show a line with an even steeper slope; such a life would be inconsistent with the natural life span. The other curves reflect the potential effects of plasticity on vitality. By utilizing the plasticity inherent in the modifiable markers of aging—including the muscular reserve, cardiac reserve, and intellectual function—the first part of the curve for the individual inevitably is displaced upward. Because of the barrier to superlongevity, the decreased slope in the early part of the curve must be compensated by a steeper slope later—a rectangular curve.

Note that there is an area of linear senescence in each curve, but the degree of slope is altered. Even with maximum function, as shown in Figure 9-2 for marathon world record times by age, there is a slow linear decline with age after age 30. Plasticity does not imply that this biologically fixed decline can be overcome. Plasticity implies that an individual not already performing near a personal maximum can improve performance at any age. Thus, plasticity applies for the vast majority of individuals and for many aspects of aging in all individuals. Note also that variation among individuals, as represented by the vertical lines at particular ages, increases with the age of the individual.

The known modifiable aging markers are listed in Table 10-1, and the list is an impressive one. The personal decisions required for expression of plasticity are largely redundant, and the implicit theme is obvious—a faculty that is unused atrophies and functions poorly. Effort and practice are required to maintain any given function. If the effort is unpleasant, a value trade-off is created, with resultant anguish over the decision.

To this list could be added a number of specific diseases, such as arteriosclerosis, emphysema, cirrhosis, probably osteoarthritis, lung cancer, hemorrhoids,

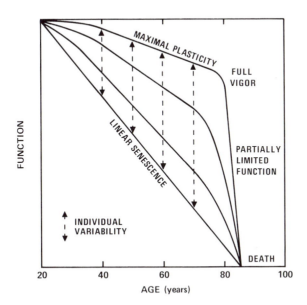

FIGURE 10-1.
The individual rectangular curves for vigor,
representing a lifetime of vigor followed by terminal
collapse.

TABLE 10-1.
Modifiable Aspects of Aging

Aging Marker	Personal Decision(s) Required
Cardiac reserve	Exercise, nonsmoking
Dental decay	Prophylaxis, diet
Glucose tolerance	Weight control, exercise, diet
Intelligence tests	Training, practice
Memory	Training, practice
Osteoporosis	Weight-bearing exercise, diet
Physical endurance	Exercise, weight control
Physical strength	Exercise
Pulmonary reserve	Exercise, nonsmoking
Reaction time	Training, practice
Serum cholesterol	Diet, weight control, exercise
Social ability	Practice
Skin aging	Sun avoidance
Systolic blood pressure	Salt limitation, weight control, exercise

diverticulitis, tension headache, gallbladder disease, and so forth. Rather than speaking of unused faculties, we would speak instead of postponement of illness. In both cases, the role of personal decision and personal effort is crucial.

Note that the argument becomes much stronger when we talk of aging markers rather than of risk factors for specific diseases, even though the personal decisions required are the same. For disease prevention, knowledge that the habit change will alter the disease is often uncertain, usually because studies are incomplete. In contrast, the ability to modify these aging markers has been definitively established.

Some other aspects of aging, such as those listed in Table 10-2, are apparently fixed biological phenomena, and attempts to modify them have not yet been successful. We emphasize also that the more numerous modifiable variables still are subject to a steady decline in optimal performance with age; they may be improved only because so few individuals are performing at their peak level. Of course, there may well be some other characteristics, such as "wisdom," which depend on accumulated experiences and which could steadily improve with age.

The postulates of a finite life span, plasticity, and the central role of personal choice in retarding aspects of aging have far-reaching implications that extend into philosophical and ethical realms. They suggest an existential construction, with triumph and despair, hope and anguish, resulting from an eternal struggle against a fixed limit.

Camus' essay on the myth of Sisyphus stands as an appropriate analogy for life against the barrier. Sisyphus was condemned, for reasons not important to this discussion, to futile and hopeless work. He was required to push a large stone, slowly and with great effort, to the top of a hill. Then, he had to let the stone roll back down the hill, return himself to the bottom of the hill, and push the stone again toward the top. And then again let the stone roll back. And again, and again.

The life of Sisyphus epitomized to Camus the absurd. The heroic effort required, the hopelessness of the task, the despair at the irrevocable sentence were all part of the anguish of Sisyphus. Yet Camus saw Sisyphus as happy, and perhaps triumphant. It was his stone. His knowledge of his plight raised him above his imprisonment. The absurdity of the predicament was really not more than that of anyone else who awoke, ate, worked, ate, worked again, went to sleep, and awoke again to repeat the same effort for a lifetime. If Sisyphus was doomed, his fate was no worse than ours, his life no more anguished. And if he could be triumphant, so then can we.

TABLE 10-2.
Nonmodifiable Aspects of Aging

Arterial wall rigidity
Cataract formation
Graying of hair
Kidney reserve
Thinning of hair
Elasticity of skin

Final victory over death, in the secular sense, is not obtainable. The choice of greater effort does not lead to permanent gains, only to a shorter period of pain. Mastery of one's own destiny is temporary and in some sense illusory. Moreover, it is essentially probabilistic. Chance may defeat the most energetic plan. Death is inevitable. But the life that precedes death may be changed, by choice, and the choices cannot be avoided. To choose not to decide is to decide. To require foreknowledge before choice is not possible. And the consequences of the decisions accrue and multiply.

It is our intention here to discuss a few of the ethical dilemmas created by current knowledge of human aging. There are no clear solutions and certainly no simple answers; indeed, the questions themselves are old ones, recast slightly by current knowledge.

THE DILEMMA OF SUICIDE

The central dilemma of Hamlet is made yet more difficult by the existence of a finite life span and declining organ reserve with age. Should life be ended before it is absolutely necessary? Is suicide ethical? Do personal choice and personal responsibility extend to what has been called "the only important question in philosophy"—to the deliberate ending of one's own life?

In an individual life following a rectangular curve of vitality, there are seemingly clear differences between suicide on the flat portion of the curve and suicide on the steep decline. Self-destruction on the sharp downslope represents only a small environmental challenge; it only substitutes for a different small perturbation that would at any rate come soon. During the terminal drop in function, there is no reserve for recovery. Earlier in life, on the flat portion of the curve, survival of a suicide attempt returns the individual to a stable level of health, with a decline in physiological function of perhaps 1% per year. In the final stages of senescence, there is no possibility of return to health, only continuation of the terminal drop.

Traditionally, suicide is held to be legally and morally wrong. Absolute ethical principles are often used as final answers to Hamlet's dilemma, perhaps correctly. Yet it is difficult to avoid the observation that suicide when return to life function is possible is different from suicide when there is no hope of such return. Absolute principles do not allow such distinctions, and relative principles are clearly required by the next dilemma.

THE DILEMMA OF RELINQUISHING YOUTH

The fact of plasticity presents a dilemma strangely analogous to that of suicide. Since personal choice can preserve physical, intellectual, and social vigor, is it ethical to choose otherwise? Is failure to take advantage of plasticity a form of self-destruction? Is the essence of life itself thus being abandoned? Granting that one can slow the rate of decay, does the choice become morally obligatory?

It is ethical to be fat? To smoke cigarettes? To be inactive? To overindulge in alcohol consumption? Not to buckle the seat belts of an automobile? Do those who are bent on self-destruction along one path or another have any real choice about their own fate? Or are they simply playing out a scenario that is predetermined by their genetic constitution, their fixed personality structure, their upbringing, or indeed their basic nature?

Such suggestions are anathema to most ethical theory, which holds that the ability to make free, uninfluenced choices is essential to human dignity and which contrasts the freedom of personal choice in democratic societies with that of more coercive authoritarian regimes. Life, liberty, and the pursuit of happiness are reserved for the individual as basic rights. And yet these arguments will not cleanly separate from those against suicide. To knowingly indulge in behavior with a statistical probability of shortening life is suspiciously similar to the act of ingesting an overdose of sleeping pills.

What happens when the right to life and the right to the pursuit of happiness become antithetical, as with a cigarette or alcohol habit? Is the anti-jogger suicidal?

We suggest that the anguish of personal choice arises from such fundamental conflicts. Greek or Shakespearean tragedy evolves slowly and majestically as a series of choices that lead inexorably to the tragic conclusion. The drama is heightened because of the magnitude of the events stemming from each choice, with the accrual of consequences insidious and inevitable.

The availability of choice makes tragedy possible; the possibility of tragedy makes choices anguished. With plasticity in aging, the choice to age more rapidly or to discipline immediate pleasures becomes terrible. The self-destructive thrills of young life come into agonizing conflict with the possibility of serene joy in older life.

THE DILEMMA OF SOCIAL EQUITY

If the problems of health and aging in our society were susceptible to political solution, personal anguish could be submerged in collective social responsibility. But our current health problems are overwhelmingly more subject to personal solutions than societal ones.

Yet society is not entirely separate from the personal decision, since rewards and punishments exist in the social structure, whether by accident or by design. Taxes on toxic products, levels of support for the unemployed or disabled, and distribution of the consequences of decisions to the general population through insurance mechanisms are examples of societal incentives that influence or even coerce individual choices. And such incentives lead to the dilemma of equity.

Should those who choose not to age rapidly pay the hospital costs of those who choose otherwise? Heavy smokers and heavy drinkers have four times the medical expenses of moderate smokers and drinkers. The obese use an average of twice as many hospital bed-days as the nonobese. The great majority of high-cost hospitalizations currently are related to recurrent episodes of ill health caused by personal habits that predictably lead to such consequences. What is social equity? Does it require the equal distribution or risk, even though this separates the financial consequences of deleterious choice from the personal decision? Or should the expected costs of decisions be distributed among those who make such decisions? Life insurance rates statistically should be much lower for active, nonsmoking, moderate drinking, slender persons. Should there be good-driver discounts or good-habit discounts for medical insurance? Should the social savings resulting from personal choices accrue to the society or to the individual making the choices? Should societal incentives that reduce the anguish of personal choice be encouraged or removed?

Serious discussion of this dilemma is impeded by an underlying dilemma, that of the actual nature of deleterious personal habits. Are they really adverse choices, or are they afflictions that are beyond individual responsibility? Is alcoholism a disease? Is obesity? Is tobacco addiction? Is physical inactivity a disease? Is sunbathing? There is little debate about the importance of these factors to aspects of health, but there is substantial confusion about their relationship to personal choice. The record of orthodox medical approaches to habit moderation is disappointing, although somewhat better results have come from group interactions of motivated individuals, such as Alcoholics Anonymous and Weight Watchers. But these groups themselves often visualize their target conditions as life-long diseases rather than as noxious personal habits.

Veatch has recently summarized rather eloquently the ethical issues surrounding voluntary risks to health, beginning with the question of whether adverse health behaviors are truly voluntary. He notes three alternate interpretations—the medical model, the psychological model, and the social structural model—and finds serious fault with each. The medical model holds that disease is the result of external and uncontrollable causation; this flies in the face of the empirical realities of chronic diseases. The psychological model in essence holds that determinism is modulated through psychological imperatives, perhaps grounded in childhood experiences, which make it impossible for an adult to change compulsive habits. Finally, the social structural model notes the association of poor health habits with lower socioeconomic class, considers the arguments of personal control to be "blaming the victim," and would have society assume the ultimate responsibility for improving the conditions that lead to better health and, in our context, delayed aging.

After inspecting these several models, it is difficult to escape Veatch's conclusions that there are influences on personal behavior from each of them but that the voluntary elements, and, for certain segments of society, the social structural elements, are the most critical. The ultimate model is multicausal and is not exclusively the property of medicine, psychology, sociology, or public policy. But when seeking to treat an individual patient or a national population, one looks for methods by which the problem may be altered. Here, one is clearly led to the questions of modifying individual behavior through medical programs and public policy, incorporating the power of personal choice for change within a social structural model. And this leads to a related dilemma.

THE DILEMMA OF PATERNALISM

The Hippocratic tradition commits the physician to doing everything possible to benefit the patient. In its strongest form, it leaves no room for personal self-determination. The patient must not smoke. The patient must lose weight. The medication must be taken. The physician gives and writes orders. The patient obeys. Thus, disease is thwarted and health restored.

Few now feel very comfortable with the authoritarian physician, and this tradition has been relaxed to a considerable degree. Yet analysis of the social causes underlying voluntary behavior can have the effect of putting public policy in the role of the Hippocratic physician. We have emphasized the social influences on personal habits that accelerate aging—lack of exercise, smoking, overeating, overdrinking. Warnings about excessive sun exposure, automobile seat belts, and passive automotive restraint systems are other examples of social action to control personal behavior. Most of us react with revulsion to the bare suggestion of regulation of such choices. Our reaction is a recognition that our free choice is threatened; it is an affirmation of the dominant role of personal choice. We do not want our choices constrained, and we are willing to trade some health benefits for this freedom.

In our view, the questions of individual choice versus social controls are more easily resolved at the level of the average person rather than at the level of the most seriously afflicted person. The question does not need to be addressed at the level of the morbidly obese or the end-stage alcoholic. The effects of habits on health are incremental and are to a considerable extent independent of the level of abuse. Increase in physical activity modifies risk factors even for those already moderately active. Lowering of cholesterol by 20% appears to convey about the same health improvement whether the reduction is from high initial levels or from moderate levels.

At less pathological levels, it seems much more appropriate to speak of habits rather than diseases and to emphasize choice rather than social control. Most of us directly experience or observe the ability to change habit patterns by personal choice. Moreover, national habit patterns change markedly for different cohorts. Cigarette smoking increases, then decreases. Hard liquor usage rises, then declines as a trend toward increased consumption of table wine emerges. New habits, such as marijuana use, emerge and become popular. Groups of people change, so individuals must also. Without ignoring the difficult ethical questions, it seems most reasonable to reaffirm the value of personal choice over social regulation of potentially harmful personal habits.

Excessive concern about inequities in the social structure evades the questions of individual responsibility and is often expressed in a manner that ignores a set of empirical realities. Positive health decisions generally are less expensive in economic terms then are negative ones. It costs money to overeat, to smoke, to drink. Most poor foods (junk food, soft drinks, heavily salted snacks) are over-priced per calorie relative to better foods. Exercise is among the least expensive of leisure activities. Since the poor and deprived are affected most strongly by additional expense, and since such individuals start from the worst health status, they have the most to gain from positive personal health decisions. The argument reduces to whether the socially deprived life is so devoid of pleasure that bad health habits are necessary to make life endurable; this argument collapses under its own weight.

The anguish of personal responsibility cannot be delegated, nor can the consequences of personal choices be avoided. We prefer, however, to use more positive terms than *anguish* and *despair,* and we would point instead to existential triumph. The principles of personal choice and individual responsibility lead to increased autonomy, greater personal control over our personal environment, and a paradigm that shifts power from an authority structure to the individual. Thus the emerging paradigm of health remains consistent with our ethical heritage and our political commitment to individual liberty.

You see, of course, if you're not a dunce,
How it went to pieces all at once,—
All at once, and nothing first,—
Just as bubbles do when they burst.

CHAPTER ELEVEN

THE
ONE-HOSS SHAY

*wherein a vigorous adulthood with a terminal collapse
is seen as a celebration of life*

Referring to the lines of verse from Oliver Wendell Holmes' poem "The Deacon's Masterpiece; or, The Wonderful 'One-Hoss Shay' " that appear on the opposite page, Lewis Thomas has written: "This is, in high metaphor, what happens when a healthy old creature, old man or old mayfly, dies. There is no outside evil force, nor any central flaw. The dying is built into the system so that it can occur at once, at the end of a preclocked, genetically determined allotment of living. Centralization ceases, the forces that used to hold cells together are disrupted, the cells lose recognition of each other, chemical signaling between cells comes to an end, vessels become plugged by thrombi and disrupt their walls, bacteria are allowed free access to tissues normally forbidden, organelles inside cells begin to break apart; nothing holds together; it is the bursting of billions of bubbles, all at once . . . what a way to go!"

"What a way to go!" A celebration of life! A long life of vigor and vitality ending suddenly, one day, on schedule. This view of natural life ending in natural death is one which we are rapidly approaching. The rectangularization of the survival curve is a fact, and we are evolving toward a "rectangular society," seemingly inexorably. The evidence for this evolution, although not final, is compelling and convincing. The disease-free society has, very quietly, nearly arrived, and the major manifestations of aging have been shown, within limits, to be modifiable.

We have emphasized the futility of the quest for immortality. The myths of the super-centenarian, of Shangri-La, and of Methuselah crumble upon close examination. Yet, in the rubble, we find hope for a meaningful kind of rejuvenation—where the maximum life span is not prolonged but the period of vitality is. Partly this will come from the postponement of the major diseases that sap our vitality, and partly it will come from our modification of the rate of the physiological and psychological aging process itself. Insights afforded by analysis of the progression of chronic diseases apply also to aging; in important ways, we age by personal habit, and we can change our habits.

A REVIEW OF HUMAN AGING

Early in adult life in both animals and humans, there begins a steady decline in homeostasis and organ reserve in many vital systems, which results in a steady logarithmic increase in the age-specific mortality rate. This important characteristic was first noted by Gompertz and has since been confirmed by many others. Strehler and Mildvan have developed a general mathematical theory to explain these relationships. At the cellular level, experiments by Hayflick and others on the aging characteristics of human fibroblast cells have found a limit to the number of times a cell can divide, thus implying that aging occurs at the level of the cell rather than being controlled by a central mechanism in the body. Although the relationship between the Hayflick limit for cell division in the laboratory and aging of intact organisms is at best tenuous, the discovery of this limit reintroduced the analogy of the one-hoss shay into the scientific investigation of aging.

Ultimately, one seeks an explanation for aging at the molecular level. What are the time-dependent changes of molecules within cells, and why do they occur? Are the molecular changes that do occur intrinsic to cells, or are they controlled by hormones or other external regulators that are released from central sites? These questions are presently unanswerable, but partial answers will arrive as techniques are improved for studying molecular events within cells. At present, there is no convincing evidence that the aging of cells is externally controlled. The most compelling molecular aging theories focus on the importance of errors in the translation of the genetic code from DNA to messenger RNA to protein. Orgel has proposed a theory whereby errors in this sequence of information transfer can lead to a time-dependent accumulation of further errors resulting in deterioration of cell function. It seems unlikely that aging results directly from a clock programmed into the genetic code; in any event, there is certainly no evidence for such a clock. Error-prone molecular machinery, on the other hand, fits very well into evolutionary theory since errors in DNA transcription produce the mutations that are acted upon by the process of natural selection. It seems possible, but is as yet unproved, that such error-prone mechanisms are responsible for aging.

THE PARADOX OF THE AVERAGE LINEAR DECLINE

One last paradox remains. Organ reserve, a measure of vitality, decreases linearly with age. Observations, first emphasized by Shock, show a linear decline in cardiac, pulmonary, renal, and other organ function with age. Yet, most of these physiological variables are readily modified in the individual; one can quite easily improve one's reserve in many organs. The paradox is that, if many individuals improved their physiological capacities, then the average values observed by Shock and others would improve, and the central fact of senescence—the average linear decline—would become an artifact.

Decline in average values for modifiable markers of aging may indeed become artifactual, yet it also represents a truth of aging. The paradox is real, but it can be resolved. There indeed is a linear decline in average organ reserve with age, probably a linear decline for all important variables, but the optimal linear decline is not the same as the line that has been measured by physiologists. As we have shown in the example of the marathon records, optimal performance also declines linearly, and it is this decline in optimal performance that represents the immutable biological law of aging.

When one measures a variable at one time in a population of individuals of differing ages, one becomes prone to the biases of the cross-sectional study. Average values of modifiable variables at a given age represent collective social habits. If body weight declines with age, it may be just the effect of loss of muscle mass due to socially conditioned decreasing activity with age. If cardiac reserve decreases, it may also just be because physical exercise has tended to lapse as one grows older. If sexual activity decreases, it may just represent unavailability of a sexual partner. From a cross-sectional study of average values, one cannot distinguish a biological decline from a decline conditioned by cultural influences.

It is highly probable that decline in most manifestations of aging may be slowed. Yet, it is a fact that no individual, no matter how fit or how disciplined, has ever broken the statistical distributions that limit longevity. Hence, the slow linear decline in optimal performance must finally accelerate at the end of life, as in the collapse of the one-hoss shay.

THE IMMORTALISTS

Predicting the future is an uncertain business at best, and the distinction between scientific prediction and science fiction is a fine one. Much printer's ink has been used and continues to be used for the promotion of theories and prophecies quite different from those we give here, and these may collectively be termed *immortalist* theories. These theories propose that man is potentially immortal, and they suggest ways in which immortality, or at least superlongevity, might be accomplished. The appeal of such proposals to the popular media is obvious, and the most absurd claims are frequently found on the front pages of lay publications.

Cryogenics societies suggest that freezing the recently deceased will allow future societies who have learned the secret of immortality to bring the individual back to eternal life. Vitamin advocates suggest that the 200-year life span requires only sufficient intake of the particular elixir. Gerovital and other magic potions are promoted as antiaging drugs. A few exercise advocates inflate the valid statements about the value of exercise into a promise of superlongevity.

Most such claims crumble upon examination. They require wild leaps of faith, and they run counter to daily experience. For example, heavy vitamin users, physically fit runners, and individuals treated with gerovital do die, and all die within the finite life span detailed in this book.

It is not possible to anticipate all future discoveries. H. G. Wells did not foresee television, and in Aldous Huxley's *Brave New World* computers are conspicuously absent. However, time travel, space travel faster than light, and regeneration of lost limbs seem less likely now than when first predicted in science fiction.

We suspect that superlongevity and immortality are at least as difficult to achieve as travel through time.

A second class of claims, somewhat more reasonable, comes from enthusiastic scientists, and these claims are based on valid observations. A recent example is the publicity surrounding the adrenal hormone dehydroepiandrosterone, or DHEA. This hormone is associated with protection from breast cancer; it causes experimental animals to remain lean and somewhat youthful and to have a longer life expectancy. The level of this hormone decreases with age in humans and in animals, thus leading some to speculate that injections of this hormone may prolong life. The problems with such speculations should be apparent to the careful reader. Life expectancy and life span are not the same thing, and many body functions decline with age without the decline being the reason for aging. An association is not a causal connection. Still, research in such areas is clearly indicated, and the possibility of success cannot be entirely discounted.

A final set of speculations acknowledges that no impact on the life span has yet been made by medical science and that the problem is one of monumental difficulty. The solutions, therefore, must involve a quantum jump in scientific knowledge and thus the possibility of entirely new approaches. Recombinant DNA techniques might perhaps offer such an opportunity. If we could understand the aging process at the cellular level and its underlying molecular mechanisms, then we might be able to alter the information units in the cells and thereby alter the life span.

In this book, we have chosen to limit our discussion to the period included by the lifetime of people already born—to ourselves rather than our descendants. Immortality or superlongevity will not accrue to us. We doubt also that they will be implemented by future societies, but, as noted, such prophecies are inherently uncertain. For present generations, however, the finite life span is a certainty. The most reasonable approaches to altering the life span involve intervention early in life or in utero, and any drugs to be employed would require many decades of long-term testing before they could be considered free of catastrophic side effects. The human life span has been constant for at least 100,000 years, and change is not at hand.

Even the speculations, we think, detract from the real and present task, which is to postpone the manifestations of aging and to improve the quality of life. These tasks are upon us now, and they present the exciting challenge of the rectangular society.

THE RECTANGULAR SOCIETY

Whatever may be the ultimate cause of aging at the molecular level, the ideal aging process for the individual is represented by a rectangular curve. As chronic diseases are postponed, and as physiological aging is slowed by research and lifestyle changes, natural life will become more prevalent. Personal choice will come to play an increasingly dominant role in health, in the prevention of premature disease, and in the favorable modification of those aspects of aging that are plastic. The result can be a "rectangular society," where the maximum life span is fixed at about 100 years, and the median life span is fixed at about 85 years.

What will life be like in a rectangular society? There will not be an accumulation of debilitated elderly people exhausting the medical and social resources of the society. On the contrary, granting a stable birth rate, there will be comparable numbers of vigorous, healthy people in each of the first seven decades of life, followed by a decline in the number of individuals between 70 and 100 years of age. Although death and debility resulting from congenital defects and accidents will always be present, and some will consciously choose not to live out a natural life through personal choice of self-destructive behavior patterns, most persons in the rectangular society will succumb to relatively short-term illnesses in the final senescent period of life; natural death will occur at the end of natural life.

The rectangular society does not represent a utopian society free from problems. The medical care delivery system must undergo a fundamental upheaval—internists will become geriatricians, and acute care hospitals will be occupied primarily by geriatric patients. Costs of medical care can fall if heroic treatment methods are abandoned in favor of more rational therapeutic approaches at home, in hospice and respite care units, in convalescent facilities, and in modified nursing homes. When people develop cardiovascular or malignant diseases in their 80's and 90's instead of their 50's and 60's, therapeutic and diagnostic decisions should be more humane and less dramatic. Natural death cannot be avoided, no matter the expenditure. Acute care hospitals as we know them today will cease to be the centerpieces of the medical care system; those that remain will focus on accidents and acute illness in those, young and old, who are vigorous. The question of euthanasia in the rectangular society will be no different than it is today; vigorous patients should receive vigorous treatment as they do now, and heroic treatment should be withheld only when the effort is foredoomed.

Present-day retirement policies will make little sense in a rectangular society. Too great a national resource is thus squandered, and the health costs of uselessness will accrue to the same older people supposedly helped by such a policy. With the postponement of chronic diseases, and with maximal plasticity in aging, most older persons will be in excellent health. Contained within the ranks of these unique people is an enormous reservoir of experience and wisdom, ideal for the accomplishment of many important tasks. Integration of these extraordinary persons into the mainstream of society through the incentives of part-time work and abandonment of arbitrary retirement laws will be essential. Picasso, Casals, Churchill, de Gaulle, Rubenstein, Basie, Heifetz, Mao, and Tito, among many others, demonstrate the potential of older people in a rectangular society. Grandma Moses was painting at 100. Bertrand Russell was publicly active at 94. George Bernard Shaw was writing at 91. Mary Baker Eddy directed the Christian Science Church at 89. Albert Schweitzer headed an African hospital at 89. Michelangelo designed churches at 88. Konrad Adenauer was the Chancellor of Germany at 88. The actual Zorba the Greek epitomized the vigor and joy of old age in his final words: "I've done heaps and heaps of things in my life, but I still did not do enough. Men like me ought to live a thousand years." The life of Zorba as presented by Kazantzakis in *Zorba the Greek* is one of the most poignant examples of vitality in old age that can be found in literature.

The integration of the older members of society into the mainstream of life is the challenge for the coming era. Free from the agony of lingering illness, filled with the vigor of natural life, the rectangular society represents a great hope for the fulfillment of human potential. The ideal rectangular society is obligated to encourage personal choice for young and old alike. Incentives favoring individual choices that promote the general welfare are essential to a rectangular society.

Of course, it may not happen. Realistically, societies have difficulties in achieving and maintaining the ideal. Man's traditional inhumanity to man remains an enduring reality. The social structure may not permit the exercise of personal choice or may continue to foster incentives opposed to natural life. Individuals or corporate greed may put profit above health. Many individuals, perhaps a majority, may opt not to preserve personal vitality; after all, it requires considerable personal effort. And we face the problem of designing social structures never seen before. Many societies have evolved the role of the patriarch, the single senior statesman of a community. But never has a society faced the problem of integrating an entire cohort of older individuals into the mainstream. This task is clearly a difficult one.

But we remain optimistic. The health and aging problems of the present time are not intractable. The postponement of chronic diseases and the retardation of aging through fundamental research and collective personal effort are realistic strategies for the near future, entirely consistent with our health gains up to the present. Extension of the life span itself is a strategy for the more distant future; we have not yet even begun to acquire the knowledge necessary to accomplish this goal. Underlying our arguments here is the axiom that the maximum human life span will remain essentially fixed for the foreseeable future, as it has in the past. We have attempted to project a realistic future consistent with present trends, one which includes only goals that are potentially within reach. Certainly we will never be completely accident free or disease free, but we may come close. Certainly any society will always contain individuals who adopt self-destructive lifestyles, but they may become a decreasing minority. Certainly a free society will always have members who lack self-discipline or the will to live a natural life. Certainly, in a more rectangular society, we will be left with a residue of premature mortality from congenital defects, accidents, and diseases of self-abuse, which will detract from the ideal. These residual problems need have no fundamental bearing on the basic characteristics of the society. In the rectangular society, the vast majority of those persons who freely choose to live a full life will be able to do so.

LIFE TABLES

The life table for a given society in a given year is constructed from the age-specific mortality rates, R_x, determined for each age x for the total population of the society. R_x is defined as the number of persons who die in the age interval x to $x + 1$ per 1000 persons who are alive at the beginning of the age interval. In other words, R_x equals the deaths per year per 1000 persons who enter age x alive.

The number of persons alive at the beginning of each age interval x to $x + 1$ is defined as L_x, and the number of persons who die during this same age interval is defined as D_x. From these definitions, it follows that

$$R_x = \frac{D_x}{L_x} \times 1000 \tag{1}$$

The life table is constructed by beginning with 100,000 live births and then applying equation (1) to determine all subsequent values of L_x and D_x from the known values of R_x, which are calculated from the census and mortality statistics of the total population. For example, for the United States in 1970, R_0, R_1, and R_2 were 20.16, 1.28, and 0.848, respectively. Starting from $L_0 = 100,000$, we have

$$D_0 = \frac{R_0 \cdot L_0}{1000} = 2016$$

Therefore,

$$L_1 = L_0 - D_0 = 97,984$$

and

$$D_1 = \frac{R_1 \cdot L}{1000} = 125$$

Similarly,

$$L_2 = L_1 - D_1 = 97,859$$

so that

$$D_2 = \frac{R_2 \cdot L_2}{1000} = 83$$

By repeating this calculation using the known values of R_x, the table is easily constructed for all values of L_x and D_x up to $x = 100$. Tables A-1 and A-2 are the life tables for the United States in the years 1910 and 1970, respectively. Figures 3-1, 3-2, and 3-3 are plotted from the data in Tables A-1 and A-2.

TABLE A-1.
Life Table for the United States, 1910

Age interval in years (x)	Number alive at beginning of age interval x (L_x)	Number dying in age interval x (D_x)	Mortality rate per 1000 during age interval x (R_x)
0–1	100,000	11,462	114.62
1–2	88,538	2,446	27.62
2–3	86,092	1,062	12.34
3–4	85,030	666	7.83
4–5	84,364	477	5.65
5–6	83,887	390	4.66
6–7	83,497	327	3.91
7–8	83,170	274	3.30
8–9	82,896	234	2.82
9–10	82,662	204	2.47
10–11	82,458	187	2.27
11–12	82,271	180	2.19
12–13	82,091	182	2.22
13–14	81,909	193	2.36
14–15	81,716	210	2.57
19–20	80,418	344	4.28
24–25	78,471	425	5.42
29–30	76,258	479	6.28
34–35	73,695	568	7.72
39–40	70,686	644	9.11
44–45	67,301	740	10.99
49–50	63,333	873	13.77
54–55	58,039	1,084	18.49
59–60	52,542	1,404	26.73
64–65	44,912	1,718	38.25
69–70	35,790	1,974	55.14
74–75	25,622	2,070	80,78
79–80	15,566	1,854	119.10
84–85	7,256	1,255	172.97
89–90	2,439	571	234.31
94–95	523	162	310.17
99–100	65	25	385.46
100–101	40	16	401.91

Source: L. I. Dublin, "The Possibility of Extending Human Life." In *The Harvey Lectures, 1921–1922,* Series XVII. Philadelphia: Lippincott, 1923, 179–205.

TABLE A-2.
Life Table for the United States, 1970

Age interval in years (x)	Number alive at beginning of age interval x (L_x)	Number dying in age interval x (D_x)	Mortality rate per 1000 during age interval x (R_x)
0–1	100,000	2,016	20.16
1–2	97,984	125	1.28
2–3	97,859	83	0.848
3–4	97,776	68	0.695
4–5	97,708	55	0.563
5–6	97,653	62	0.635
6–7	97,591	49	0.502
7–8	97,542	38	0.390
8–9	97,504	30	0.308
9–10	97,474	26	0.267
10–11	97,448	25	0.257
11–12	97,423	28	0.287
12–13	97,395	36	0.370
13–14	97,359	47	0.483
14–15	97,312	62	0.637
19–20	96,843	128	1.32
24–25	96,145	143	1.49
29–30	95,454	142	1.49
34–35	94,675	184	1.94
39–40	93,600	270	2.88
44–45	91,995	410	4.46
49–50	89,559	614	6.86
54–55	85,969	900	10.47
59–60	80,730	1,272	15.76
64–65	73,560	1,702	23.14
69–70	64,077	2,179	34.01
74–75	52,308	2,644	50.55
79–80	38,279	2,945	76.94
84–85	23,805	2,728	114.60
89–90	11,387	1,924	169.00
94–95	3,927	888	226.00
99–100	921	265	288.00
100–101	656	197	300.00

Source: *Vital Statistics of the United States,* National Center for Health Statistics, 1970.

APPENDIX B

GOMPERTZ'S LAW

In 1825, the English actuary Benjamin Gompertz published his classic paper on the nature of human mortality. From his observations of the life tables of four different population groups (Northampton, Deparcieux, Sweden, and Carlisle), Gompertz discovered a general empirical mathematical relationship between L_x and x, where L_x is the number of persons living at age x. This relationship took the form

$$ln\ L_x = q^x\ lng\ +\ lnd \tag{1}$$

or

$$L_x = d \cdot (g)^{q^x}$$

where d, g, and q are constants characteristic of each population. This relationship can be rewritten as

$$\ln L_x = \frac{-R_0}{a} e^{ax} + \ln d \qquad (1a)$$

where $q = e^a$ and $\ln g = -R_0/a$, allowing the constants e, R_0, and a to replace the constants g and q. Thus

$$\frac{-d \ln L_x}{dx} = R_0 e^{ax}$$

But

$$\frac{-d \ln L_x}{dx} = \frac{-d L_x/dx}{L_x} = R_x = \text{age-specific mortality rate}$$

Thus

$$R_x = R_0 e^{ax} \qquad (2)$$

Equation 2 is often referred to as Gompertz's law, where the age-specific mortality rate, R_x, increases exponentially with age x. Gompertz's law can be rewritten as

$$\ln R_x = ax + \ln R_0 \qquad (3)$$

Thus, if the logarithm of R_x is plotted against age x as in Figure 3-3, a straight line will occur for those ages where the law is valid (usually greater than 30 years).

Gompertz was aware that death may occur from several types of causes, as expressed in his statement, "It is possible that death may be the consequence of two generally co-existing causes; the one, chance, without previous disposition to death or deterioration; the other, a deterioration, or an increased inability to withstand destruction." Makeham modified Gompertz's law to take into account the first type of chance deaths, which are independent of age, by adding a constant term, denoted A. Thus, the Gompertz–Makeham expression takes the form

$$R_x = R_0 e^{ax} + A \qquad (4)$$

For wild animals and primitive human societies, the second term, A, representing chance deaths, is dominant. Under these conditions,

$$R_x = \frac{-d \ln L_x}{dx} = A$$

and therefore

$$L_x = L_0 e^{-ax} \qquad (5)$$

so that L_x describes a simple exponential decay curve.

THE
STREHLER–MILDVAN
THEORY OF AGING

The first postulate of the Strehler–Mildvan theory is that the age-specific mortality rate, R_x, is proportional to the frequency of environmental challenges, F_x, which are sufficient to cause the death of an organism of age x. Thus

$$R_x = cF_x \qquad (1)$$

where c is a constant.

The second postulate is that

$$F_x = k e^{-V_x/bD} \qquad (2)$$

where k and b are constants, V_x is the vitality of the organism at age x, and D is related to the deleteriousness of the environment. V_x is related to the total organ reserve of an organism at age x and is equal to the size of an environmental challenge sufficient to cause death. The term bD is the average size of environmental stress fluctuation. Note that F_x, and consequently R_x, decreases as V_x increases and D decreases.

From Appendix B, the Gompertz equation describing the mortality rate is

$$R_x = R_0 e^{ax} \tag{3}$$

Combining equations (1), (2), and (3), we have

$$R_0 e^{ax} = c\,k\,e^{-V_x/bD} = K e^{-V_x/bD} \tag{4}$$

Solving for V_x, we obtain

$$V_x = bD\ln K/R_0 \left(1 - \frac{ax}{\ln K/R_0} \right)$$

or

$$V_x = V_0 (1 - Bx) \tag{5}$$

where

$$V_0 = bD\ln K/R_0 \text{ and } B = \frac{a}{\ln K/R_0}$$

Thus the Strehler–Mildvan theory predicts that vitality, V_x, decreases linearly with age, x, while the age-specific mortality rate, R_x, increases exponentially.

REFERENCES

CHAPTER ONE

Comfort, A. *The Biology of Senescence,* Third Edition. New York: Elsevier, 1979.

Comfort, A. "Longer Life by 1990?" *New Scientist* 11 Dec. 1969.

Fries, J. F. "Aging, Natural Death, and the Compression of Morbidity." *New England Journal of Medicine* 1980, 303:130–135.

Fries, J. F., and Ehrlich, G. E., eds. *Prognosis: Contemporary Outcomes of Disease.* Bowie, Md.: Charles Press, 1980.

Fuchs, V. R. *Who Shall Live? Health, Economics, and Social Choice.* New York: Basic Books, 1974.

Gordon, T. J., Gerjuoy, H., and Anderson, M., eds. *Life-Extending Technologies: A Technology Assessment.* Elmsford, N.Y.: Pergamon Press, 1977. (Pergamon Policy Studies.)

Knowles, J. H., ed. *Doing Better and Feeling Worse: Health in the United States.* New York: Norton, 1977.

McKeown, T. *The Role of Medicine: Dream, Mirage or Nemesis?* Princeton: Princeton University Press, 1979.

Murphy, E. A. *The Logic of Medicine.* Baltimore: The Johns Hopkins University Press, 1976.

Preston, S. H. *Mortality Patterns in National Populations.* New York: Academic Press, 1976.

Riley, M. W. *Aging from Birth to Death: Interdisciplinary Perspectives.* Boulder: Westview Press, 1979.

Totman, R. *Social Causes of Illness.* New York: Pantheon Books, 1979.

Vickery, D., and Fries, J. F. *Take Care of Yourself.* Reading, Mass.: Addison-Wesley, 1976.

CHAPTER TWO

Davis, D. *The Centenarians of the Andes.* Garden City, N.Y.: Anchor Press, 1975.

De Busk, F. L. "The Hutchinson–Gilford Progeria Syndrome." *Journal of Pediatrics* 1972, 80 (2):697–724.

Epstein, C. J., et al. "Werner's Syndrome." *Medicine* 1966, 45:177–221.

Gruman, G. J. "A History of Ideas About the Prolongation of Life." *Transactions of the American Philosophical Society* 1966, 56 (9):1–102.

Leaf, A. "Every Day Is a Gift When You Are over 100." *National Geographic* 1973, 143:93–110.

Leaf, A. "Getting Old." *Scientific American* 1973, 229:45–52.

Leaf, A. "Unusual Longevity—The Common Denominator." *Hospital Practice* 1973, 8:75–86.

Leaf, A. *Youth in Old Age.* New York: McGraw-Hill, 1975.

McCay, C. M., Crowell, M. F., and Maynard, L. A. "The Effect of Retarded Growth upon the Length of the Life Span and upon the Ultimate Body Size." *Journal of Nutrition* 1935, 10:63.

McCay, C. M., Sperling, G., and Barnes, L. L. "Growth, Aging, Chronic Diseases, and Life Span in Rats." *Archives of Biochemistry* 1943, 2:469–479.

McCay, C. M., et al. "Retarded Growth, Life Span, Ultimate Body Size, and Age Changes in the Albino Rat After Feeding Diets Restricted in Calories." *Journal of Nutrition* 1939, 18:1–13.

Mazess, R. B., and Forman, S. H. "Longevity and Age Exaggeration in Vilcabamba, Ecuador." *Journal of Gerontology* 1979, 34:94–98.

Medvedev, Z. A. "Aging and Longevity—New Approaches and New Prospectives." *Gerontologist* 1975, 15:196–201.

Medvedev, Z. A. "Caucasus and Altay Longevity—A Biological or Social Problem." *Gerontologist* 1974, 14:381–387.

Packer, L., and Smith, J. R. Extension of the Lifespan of Cultured Normal Human Diploid Cells by Vitamin E. *Proceedings of the National Academy of Sciences* 1974, 71:4763–4767; 1977, 74:1640–1641.

Ross, M. H. "Length of Life and Nutrition in the Rat." *Journal of Nutrition* 1961, 75:197–210.

Ross, M. H., Lustbader, E., and Bras, G. "Dietary Practices and Growth Responses as Predictions of Longevity." *Nature* 1976, 262:548–553.

Thomas, L. "Medical Lessons from History." In *The Medusa and the Snail*. New York: Viking Press, 1979, 158–175.

CHAPTER THREE

Bernard, C. *An Introduction to the Study of Experimental Medicine*. New York: Macmillan, 1957.

Bernard, C. *Lectures on the Phenomena of Life Common to Animals and Plants*. Springfield: Thomas, 1974. (Originally published in France in 1878.)

Cannon, W. B. *The Wisdom of the Body*. New York: Norton, 1932.

Comfort, A. *The Biology of Senescence,* Third Edition. New York: Elsevier, 1979.

Cutler, R. G. "Evolution of Human Longevity and the Genetic Complexity Governing Aging Rate." *Proceedings of the National Academy of Sciences* 1975, 72:4664–4668.

Cutler, R. G. "Evolution of Human Longevity: A Critical Overview." *Mechanisms of Aging and Development* 1979, 9:337–354.

Dubos, R. *Man Adapting*. New Haven: Yale University Press, 1965.

Gompertz, B. "On the Nature of the Function Expressive of the Law of Human Mortality." *Philosophical Transactions of the Royal Society of London* 1825, I:513–585.

Greenwood, M. "Laws of Mortality from the Biological Point of View." *Journal of Hygiene* 1928, 28:267–294.

Greenwood, M., and Irwin, J. O. "The Biostatistics of Senility." *Human Biology* 1939, 11:1–23.

Henderson, R. In *Mortality Laws and Statistics*. New York: Wiley, 1915, p. 27.

Kohn, R. R. *Principles of Mammalian Aging,* Second Edition. Englewood Cliffs, N.J.: Prentice-Hall, 1978.

Martin, G. M. "Genetic and Evolutionary Aspects of Aging." *Federation of American Societies for Experimental Biology* 1979, 38:1962–1967.

Masoro, E. J., et al. "Analysis and Exploration of Age-Related Changes in Mammalian Structure and Function." *Federation Proceedings* 1979, 38:1956–1961.

Platt, R. "Reflections on Aging and Death." *Lancet* 1963, I:1–6.

Riley, M. W. *Aging from Birth to Death: Interdisciplinary Perspectives.* Boulder: Westview Press, 1979.

Sacher, G. C. "Life Table Modification and Life Prolongation." In L. Hayflick and C. E. Finch, eds., *Handbook of the Biology of Aging.* New York: Van Nostrand Reinhold, 1977, 582–638.

Sacher, G. C. "Longevity and Aging in Vertebrate Evolution." *BioScience* 1978, 28:497–501.

Samorajski, T. "How the Human Brain Responds to Aging." *Journal of the American Geriatric Society* 1976, 24:4–11.

Shock, N. "Systems Integration." In L. Hayflick and C. E. Finch, eds., *Handbook of the Biology of Aging.* New York: Van Nostrand Reinhold, 1977, 639–665.

Strehler, B. L. *Time, Cells, and Aging,* Second Edition. New York: Academic Press, 1977.

Strehler, B. L., and Mildvan, A. S. "General Theory of Mortality and Aging." *Science* 1960, 132:14–21.

Upton, A. C. "Pathobiology." In L. Hayflick and C. E. Finch, eds., *Handbook of the Biology of Aging.* New York: Van Nostrand Reinhold, 1977, 513–535.

Waring, J. *The Middle Years: A Multidisciplinary View.* New York: Academy for Educational Development, 1978.

Young V. R. "Diet as a Modulator of Aging and Longevity." *Federation Proceedings* 1979, 38:1994–2000.

CHAPTER FOUR

Bell, E., et al. "Loss of Division Potential in Vitro: Aging or Differentiation?" *Science* 1978, 202:1158–1163.

Comfort, A. *The Biology of Senescence,* Third Edition. New York: Elsevier, 1979.

Cristofalo, V. J., and Rosner, B. A. "Modulation of Cell Proliferation and Senescence of WI-38 Cells by Hydrocortisone." *Federation Proceedings* 1979, 38:1851–1856.

Edelman, P., and Gallent, J. "On the Translational Error Theory of Aging." *Proceedings of the National Academy of Sciences* 1977, 74:33–96.

Goldstein, S. "Aging in Vitro." *Experimental Cell Research* 1974:83:297.

Goldstein, S. "Senescence." In L. J. DeGroot et al., eds., *Endocrinology,* Vol. 3. New York: Grune & Stratton, 1979.

Goldstein, S., and Harley, C. B. "In Vitro Studies of Age-Associated Diseases." *Federation Proceedings* 1979, 38:1862.

Grant, R. L. "Concepts of Aging—A Historical Review." *Perspectives in Biology and Medicine* 1963, 6:443.

Harley, C. B., and Goldstein, S. "Retesting the Commitment Theory of Cellular Aging." *Science* 1980, 207:191.

Hayflick, L. "The Cell Biology of Human Aging." *New England Journal of Medicine* 1976, 295:1302–1308.

Hayflick, L. "The Cell Biology of Human Aging." *Scientific American* 1980, 242:58–65.

Hayflick, L. "The Cellular Basis for Biological Aging." In L. Hayflick and C. E. Finch, eds., *Handbook of the Biology of Aging.* New York: Van Nostrand Reinhold, 1977, 159–186.

Hayflick, L. "The Limited in Vitro Lifetime of Human Diploid Cell Strains." *Experimental Cell Research* 1965, 37:614–636.

Hayflick, L. and Moorhead, P. S. "The Serial Cultivation of Human Diploid Cell Strains." *Experimental Cell Research* 1961, 25:585.

Hirsch, G. P., et al. "Species Comparison of Protein Synthesis Accuracy. In C. Brek, C. M. Fenoglio, and D. W. King, eds., *Aging, Cancer and Cell Membranes.* New York: Thriene-Stratton: *Advances in Pathology* 1980, 7:142–159.

Hoffman, G. W. "On the Origin of the Genetic Code and the Stability of the Translation Apparatus." *Journal of Molecular Biology* 1974, 86:349.

Holliday, R., et al. "Testing the Commitment Theory of Cellular Aging." *Science* 1977, 198:366.

Hornsby, P. J., and Gill, G. N. "Loss of Division Potential in Culture: Aging or Differentiation." *Science* 1980, 208:1482–1483.

Kirkwood, T. B. L. "Evolution of Aging." *Nature* 1977, 270:301.

Kirkwood, T. B. L., and Holliday, R. "Commitment to Senescence—A Model for the Finite and Infinite Growth of Diploid Fibroblasts in Culture." *Journal of Theoretical Biology* 1975, 53:481.

Kirkwood, T. B. L., and Holliday, R. "The Stability of the Translation Apparatus." *Journal of Molecular Biology* 1975, 97:257.

Lints, F. A. "Genetics and Aging." In *Interdisciplinary Topics in Gerontology,* Vol. 14. New York: Karger, 1978.

Martin, G. M. "Cellular Aging—Clonal Senescence." *American Journal of Pathology* 1977, 89:484, 513.

Martin, G. M., Sprague, C. A., and Epstein, C. J. "Replicative Life-Span of Cultivated Human Cells." *Laboratory Investigation* 1970, 23:86.

Medawar, P. B. *An Unsolved Problem in Biology.* London: Lewis, 1952.

Orgel, L. E. "Aging of Clones of Mammalian Cells." *Nature* 1973, 243:441.

Orgel, L. E. "The Maintenance of the Accuracy of Protein Synthesis and Its Relevance to Aging." *Proceedings of the National Academy of Sciences* 1963, 49:517; 1970, 67:1496.

Rothstein, M. "Aging and the Alteration of Enzymes: A Review." *Mechanisms of Ageing and Development* 1975, 4:325–338.

Schneider, E. L., and Mitsui, Y. "The Relationship Between in Vitro Cellular Aging and in Vivo Human Age." *Proceedings of the National Academy of Sciences* 1976, 73:3584.

Siegel, R. C. "Lysyl Oxidase." *International Review of Connective Tissue Research* 1979, 8:73–118.

Smith, J. R., and Whitney, R. G. "Intraclonal Variation in Proliferative Potential of Human Diploid Fibroblasts—Stochastic Mechanism for Cellular Aging." *Science* 1980, 207:82.

Stanley, J. F., Pye, D., and MacGregor, A. "Comparison of Doubling Numbers Attained by Cultured Animal Cells with Life Span of Species." *Nature* 1975, 255:158–159.

Szilard, L. "On the Nature of the Aging Process." *Proceedings of the National Academy of Sciences* 1959, 45:30.

CHAPTER FIVE

Dublin, L. I. "The Possibility of Extending Human Life." In *The Harvey Lectures, 1921–1922,* Series XVII. Philadelphia: Lippincott, 1923, 179–205.

Fries, J. F., and Ehrlich, G. E., eds. *Prognosis: Contemporary Outcomes of Disease.* Bowie, Md.: The Charles Press, 1980.

Glassroth, J. Robins, A. G., and Snider, D. E. "Tuberculosis in the 1980's." *New England Journal of Medicine* 1980, 302:1441–1450.

McKeown, T. *The Role of Medicine.* Princeton: Princeton University Press, 1979.

National Center for Health Statistics. *Health in the United States, 1978.* Hyattsville, Md.: Office of the Assistant Secretary for Health, Public Health Service, National Center for Health Statistics. (DHEW Publication PHS 78–1232)

National Center for Health Statistics. *Health in the United States, 1979.* Hyattsville, Md.: Office of the Assistant Secretary for Health, Public Health Service, National Center for Health Statistics. (DHEW Publication PHS 80–1232)

Pearl, R. "Interrelations of the Biometric and Experimental Methods of Acquiring Knowledge: With Special Reference to the Problem of the Duration of Life." In *The Harvey Lectures, 1922–1923,* Series XVIII. Philadelphia: Lippincott, 1924, 46–71.

Upton, A. C. "Pathobiology." In L. Hayflick and C. E. Finch, eds., *Handbook of the Biology of Aging.* New York: Van Nostrand Reinhold, 1977, 513–535.

CHAPTER SIX

National Center for Health Statistics. *Health in the United States, 1978.* Hyattsville, Md.: Office of the Assistant Secretary, Public Health Service, National Center for Health Statistics. (DHEW Publication PHS 78–1232)

National Center for Health Statistics. *Vital Statistics of the United States, 1977,* Volume 2, Section 5. Hyattsville, Md.: National Center for Health Statistics, 1980. (DHEW Publication PHS 80–1104)

Newsholme, A. "National Changes in Health and Longevity." In *The Harvey Lectures, 1920–1921,* Series XVI. Philadelphia: Lippincott, 1922, 124–162.

Shock, N. W. "Discussion on Mortality and Measurement." In B. L. Strehler et al., eds., *The Biology of Aging, A Symposium.* Washington, D.C.: American Institute of Biological Sciences, 1960.

Upton, A. C. "Pathobiology." In L. Hayflick and C. E. Finch, eds., *Handbook of the Biology of Aging.* New York: Van Nostrand Reinhold, 1977, 513–535.

CHAPTER SEVEN

Breslow, L. "A Positive Strategy for the Nation's Health." *Journal of the American Medical Association* 1979, 242:2093–2095.

Cairns, J. *Cancer: Science and Society.* San Francisco: W. H. Freeman and Company, 1978.

Cohen, C. I., and Cohen, E. J. "Health Education: Panacea, Pernicious or Pointless?" *New England Journal of Medicine* 1978, 299:718–720.

Farquhar, J. W. *The American Way of Life Need Not Be Hazardous to Your Health.* New York: Norton, 1978.

Farquhar, J. W. "The Community-Based Model of Life Style Intervention Trials." *American Journal of Epidemiology* 1978, 108:103–111.

Fries, J. F. "Aging, Natural Death, and the Compression of Morbidity." *New England Journal of Medicine* 1980, 303:130–135.

Fries, J. F., and Ehrlich, G. E., eds. *Prognosis: Contemporary Outcomes of Disease.* Bowie, Md.: The Charles Press, 1980.

Gordon, T. J., Gerjuoy, H., and Anderson, M., eds. *Life-Extending Technologies: A Technology Assessment.* New York: Pergamon Press, 1979.

McKeown, T. *The Role of Medicine.* Princeton: Princeton University Press, 1979.

Mann, G. V. "Diet–Heart: End of an Era." *New England Journal of Medicine* 1977, 297:644–649.

National Center for Health Statistics. *Health in the United States, 1978.* Hyattsville, Md.: Office of the Assistant Secretary, Public Health Service, National Center for Health Statistics. (DHEW Publication PHS 78–1232)

Neugarten, B. L., and Havighurst, R. J. *Extending the Human Life Span: Social Policy and Social Ethics.* (National Science Foundation.) Washington, D.C.: U.S. Government Printing Office, 1977. (Stock No. 038–000–00337–2)

Rogers, D. E., and Blendon, R. J. "The Changing American Health Scence: Sometimes Things Get Better." *Journal of the American Medical Association* 1977, 237:1710–1714.

Seligman, M. E. P. *Helplessness: On Depression, Development, and Death.* San Francisco: W. H. Freeman and Company, 1975.

Stachnik, T. J. "Priorities for Psychology in Medical Education and Health Care Delivery." *American Psychologist* 1980, 35:8–15.

Stallones, R. A. "The Decline and Fall of Ischemic Heart Disease." Paper presented at the Annual Meeting of the Institute of Medicine, Washington, D.C., October 24, 1979.

Thomas, C. B., Santora, P. B., and Shaffer, J. W. "Health of Physicians in Midlife in Relation to Use of Alcohol: A Prospective Study of a Cohort of Former Medical Students." *Johns Hopkins Medical Journal* 1980, 146:1–10.

Valliant, G. E. "Health Consequences of Adaptation to Life." *American Journal of Medicine* 1979, 67:732–734.

Walker, W. J. "Changing United States Life-Style and Declining Vascular Mortality: Cause or Coincidence." *New England Journal of Medicine* 1977, 297:163–165.

CHAPTER EIGHT

Adner, M., and Castelli, W. "Elevated High-Density Lipoprotein Levels in Marathon Runners." *Journal of the American Medical Association* 1980, 243:534–536.

Ahrens, E. H. "Dietary Fats and Coronary Heart Disease: Unfinished Business." *Lancet* 1979, 2:1345–1348.

AMA Council on Scientific Affairs. "Smoking and Health." *Journal of the American Medical Association* 1980, 243:779–781.

Bortz, W. "Effect of Exercise on Aging—Effect of Aging on Exercise." *Journal of the American Geriatric Society* 1980, 28:49–51.

Build and Blood Pressure Study, 1959. Chicago Society of Actuaries, 1959, Vol. 1, pp. 1–268.

Drenick, E. J., et al. "Excessive Mortality and Causes of Death in Morbidly Obese Men." *Journal of the American Medical Association* 1980, 243:443–445.

"Editorial: The Pressure to Treat." *Lancet* 1980, 1:1283–1284.

"Editorial: Why the American Decline in Coronary Heart Disease?" *Lancet* 1980, 1:183–184.

Halley, S. B., et al. "Epidemiology as a Guide to Clinical Decisions: The Association Between Triglyceride and Coronary Heart Disease." *New England Journal of Medicine* 1980, 302:1383–1389.

Hartung, G., et al. "Relation of Diet to High-Density Lipoprotein Cholesterol in Middle-Aged Marathon Runners, Joggers, and Inactive Men." *New England Journal of Medicine* 1980, 302:357–361.

Havel, R. J. "High-Density Lipoproteins, Cholesterol Transport, and Coronary Heart Disease." *Circulation* 1979, 60:1–3.

Haynes, S. G., and Feinleib, M. "Women, Work and Coronary Heart Disease: Prospective Findings from the Framingham Heart Study." *American Journal of Public Health* 1980, 70:133–141.

Haynes, S. G., Feinleib, M., and Kannel, W. B. "The Relationship of Psychological Factors to Coronary Heart Disease in the Framingham Study, III: Eight-Year Incidence of Coronary Heart Disease." *American Journal of Epidemiology* 1980, 111:37–58.

Haynes, S. G., et al. "The Relationship of Psychosocial Factors to Coronary Heart Disease in the Framingham Study, I: Methods and Risk Factors." *American Journal of Epidemiology* 1978, 107:362–383.

Hypertension Detection and Follow-Up Program Cooperative Group. "Five-Year Findings of the Hypertension Detection and Follow-Up Program, I: Reduction of Mortality of Persons with High Blood Pressure, Including Mild Hypertension." *Journal of the American Medical Association* 1979, 242:2562–2571.

Kannel, W. B., Castelli, W., and Gordon, T. "Cholesterol in the Prediction of Atherosclerotic Disease—New Perspectives Based on the Framingham Study." *Annals of Internal Medicine* 1979, 90:85–91.

Kannel, W. B., and Thorn, T. J. "Implications of the Recent Decline in Cardiovascular Mortality." *Cardiovascular Medicine* 1979, 4:983–997.

Kozararevic, D., et al. "Frequency of Alcohol Consumption and Morbidity and Mortality." *Lancet* 1980, 1:613–616.

Kramsch, D., et al. "Cardiovascular Effects of Exercise in Primate Atherosclerosis." *Circulation* 1979, 60:652.

McKeown, T. *The Role of Medicine—Dream, Mirage, or Nemesis.* Princeton: Princeton University Press, 1979.

Management Committee. "The Australian Therapeutic Trial in Mild Hypertension." *Lancet* 1980, 1:1261–1267.

Mann, G. V. "The Influence of Obesity on Health." *New England Journal of Medicine* 1974, 291:178–185, 226–232.

"New Weight Standards for Men and Women." *Metropolitan Life Insurance Company Statistical Bulletin* 1959, 40:1–4.

Paffenbarger, R. S., et al. "Energy Expenditure, Cigarette Smoking, and Blood Pressure Level as Related to Death from Specific Diseases." *American Journal of Epidemiology* 1978, 108:12–18.

Paffenbarger, R. S., Wing, A. L., and Hyde, R. T. "Physical Activity as an Index of Heart Attack Risks in College Alumni." *American Journal of Epidemiology* 1978, 108:161–175.

Pedersen, D., Beck-Nielsen, H., and Hedin, L. "Increased Insulin Receptors After Exercise in Patients with Insulin-Dependent Diabetes." *New England Journal of Medicine* 1980, 302:886–892.

Rabkin, S., Mathewson, F., Ping-Hua. "Relation of Body Weight to Development of Ischemic Heart Disease in a Cohort of Young North American Men After a 26 Year Observation Period: The Manitoba Study." *American Journal of Cardiology* 1977, 39:452–458.

Relman, A. S. "Mild Hypertension—No More Benign Neglect." *New England Journal of Medicine* 1980, 302:293–294.

Soman, V., et al. "Increased Insulin Sensitivity and Insulin Binding to Monocytes After Physical Training." *New England Journal of Medicine* 1979, 1200–1204.

Sorlie, P., Gordon, T., and Kannel, W. "Body Build and Mortality—The Framingham Study." *Journal of the American Medical Association* 1980, 243:1828–1831.

Stern, M. P. "The Recent Decline in Ischemic Heart Disease Mortality." *Annals of Internal Medicine* 1979, 91:630–640.

Tall, A., and Small, D. "Plasma High-Density Lipoproteins. *New England Journal of Medicine* 1978, 299:1232–1236.

Veterans Administration Cooperative Study Group. "Effects of Treatment on Morbidity in Hypertention—Results in Patients with Diastolic Blood Pressure Averaging 115 Through 129 mm Hg." *Journal of the American Medical Association* 1967, 202:116–122.

Veterans Administration Cooperative Study Group. "Effects of Treatment on Morbidity in Hypertension—Results in Patients with Diastolic Blood Pressure Averaging 90 Through 114 mm Hg." *Journal of the American Medical Association* 1970, 213:1143–1152.

Wood, P. D., et al. "Plasma Lipoprotein Distribution in Male and Female Runners." *Annals of the New York Academy of Sciences* 1977, 301:748–763.

CHAPTER NINE

Baltes, P. B., and Baltes, M. M. "Plasticity and Variability in Psychological Aging: Methodological and Theoretical Issues." In *Determining the Effects of Aging on the Central Nervous System.* Berlin: Schering, 1980.

Baltes, P. B., and Schaie, K. W. "On the Plasticity of Intelligence in Adulthood and Old Age: Where Horn and Donaldson Fail." *American Psychologist* 1976, 31:720–725.

Beck, C. H. M. "Functional Implications of Changes in the Senescent Brain: A Review." *Journal Canadian des Sciences Neurologiques* 1978, 5:417–424.

Birren, J. E., and Wall, P. D. "Age Changes in Conduction Velocity, Refractory Periods, Number of Fibers, Connective Tissue Space, and Blood Vessels in Sciatic Nerve of Rats." *Journal of Comparative Neurology* 1956, 104:1–16.

Blumenthal, H. T. "Aging: Biologic or Pathologic?" *Hospital Practice* 1978, April, 127–137.

Comfort, A. *The Biology of Senescence,* Third Edition. New York: Elsevier, 1979.

Dehn, M. M., and Bruce, R. A. "Longitudinal Variations in Maximal Oxygen Uptake with Age and Activity." *Journal of Applied Physiology* 1972, 33:805–807.

Finch, C. E. "The Regulation of Physiological Changes During Mammalian Aging." *Quarterly Review of Biology* 1976, 51:49–83.

Finch, C. E. "The Orderly Decay of Order in the Regulation of Aging Processes." In F. E. Yates, ed., *Self-Organizing Systems: Physical, Mathematical, and Biological Viewpoints,* forthcoming.

Hartung, G. H., et al. "Relation of Diet to High-Density-Lipoprotein Cholesterol in Middle-Aged Marathon Runners, Joggers, and Inactive Men." *New England Journal of Medicine* 1980, 302:357–361.

Horn, J. L., and Donaldson, G. "Faith Is Not Enough: A Response to the Baltes–Schaie Claim That Intelligence Does Not Wane." *American Psychologist* 1977, 32:369–373.

Lahmann, H. J., Muche, H., and Schutt, M. "Refractory Period of Human Sural Nerve Action Potential Related to Age in Healthy Probands." *European Neurology* 1977, 15:85–93.

Langer, E. J., et al. "Environmental Determinants of Memory Improvement in Late Adulthood." *Journal of Personality and Social Psychology* 1979, 37:2003–2013.

Langer, E. J., and Rodin, J. "The Effects of Choice and Enhanced Personal Responsibility for the Aged: A Field Experiment in an Institutional Setting." *Journal of Personality and Social Psychology* 1976, 34:191–198.

Loftus, E. F., and Loftus, G. R. "On the Permanence of Stored Information in the Human Brain." *American Psychologist* 1980, 35:408–420.

Nesselroade, J. F., Schaie, K. W., and Baltes, P. B. "Ontogenetic and Generational Components of Structural and Quantitative Change in Adult Behavior." *Journal of Gerontology* 1972, 27:222–228.

Plemons, J. K., Willis, S. L., and Baltes, P. B. "Modifiability of Fluid Intelligence in Aging: A Short-Term Longitudinal Training Approach." *Journal of Gerontology* 1978, 33:224–231.

Pollock, M. L., Miller, H. S., and Wilmore, J. "Physiological Characteristics of Champion American Track Athletes 40 to 75 Years of Age." *Journal of Gerontology* 1974, 29:645–649.

Riley, M. W. "Aging, Social Change, and the Power of Ideas." *Daedalus* 1978, 107:39–52.

Rodin, J., and Janis, I. L. "The Social Power of Health-Care Practitioners as Agents of Change." *Journal of Social Issues* 1979, 35:60–81.

Rodin, J., and Langer, E. J. "Long-Term Effects of a Control-Relevant Intervention with the Institutionalized Aged." *Journal of Personality and Social Psychology* 1977, 35:897–902.

Schulz, R., and Hanusa, B. H. "Long-Term Effects of Control and Predictability-Enhancing Interventions: Findings and Ethical Issues." *Journal of Personality and Social Psychology* 1978, 36:1194–1201.

Seligman, M. E. P. *Helplessness: On Depression, Development, and Death.* San Francisco: W. H. Freeman and Company, 1975.

Spierer, H. *Major Transitions in the Human Life Cycle.* New York: Academy for Educational Development, 1977.

Spirduso, W. W. "Reaction and Movement Time as a Function of Age and Physical Activity Level." *Journal of Gerontology* 1975, 30:435–440.

Spirduso, W. W. "Physical Fitness, Aging, and Psychomotor Speed: A Review." *Journal of Gerontology* 1980, 35:850–865.

Spirduso, W. W., and Clifford, P. "Replication of Age and Physical Activity Effects on Reaction and Movement Time." *Journal of Gerontology* 1978, 33:26–30.

Totman, R. *Social Causes of Illness.* New York: Pantheon Books, 1979.

Valliant, G. E. "Natural History of Male Psychological Health: Effects of Mental Health on Physical Health." *New England Journal of Medicine* 1979, 301:1249–1254.

Waring, J. *The Middle Years: A Multidisciplinary View.* New York: Academy for Educational Development, 1978.

CHAPTER TEN

Baer, L. S. *Let the Patient Decide*. Philadelphia: Westminster Press, 1978.

Camus, Albert. *The Myth of Sisyphus*. New York: Random House, 1955.

Silver, Richard T. "The Dying Patient: A Clinician's View." *American Journal of Medicine* 1980, 68:473–475.

Veatch, Robert M. "Voluntary Risks to Health: The Ethical Issues." *Journal of the American Medical Association* 1980, 243:50–55.

CHAPTER ELEVEN

Holmes, O. W. "The Deacon's Masterpiece; or, The Wonderful 'One-Hoss Shay.' " From *The Autocrat of the Breakfast Table, 1857–1858*. In *The Complete Poetical Works of Oliver Wendell Holmes*. Boston: Houghton Mifflin, 1908.

Thomas, L. "The Deacon's Masterpiece." In *The Medusa and the Snail*. New York: Viking Press, 1979, 130–136.

INDEX

Abkhazia, 13
Accidents, 63, 66, 98
  motor vehicle, 38, 66
Adam, 17
Additives, 100
Adenauer, Konrad, 141
Advantages, selective, 39
Age exaggeration, 12–15
Age-dependent, 121
Aging, 1, 43, 107
  molecular, 54
  plasticity of, 91, 107–121, 125, 127
Aging genes, 40
Aging markers, 110, 126
Air pollution, 90
Alcohol abuse, 85, 86, 87, 101, 130
Alcohol consumption, 105
Alcoholics Anonymous, 130
Altruism, 119
Alveolar septal walls, 82
Ancestors, hunter–gatherers, 100

Aneurysm, 80
Angina pectoris, 80, 81
Anguish of personal responsibility, 132
Antismoking campaigns, 90
Appendicitis, 98
Aristotle, 44
Arterial degeneration, 84
Arterial insufficiency, 81
Arterial wall rigidity, 127
Arteries, 84
Arteriograms, 80
Arthritis, 79
Asbestos, 88
Atherosclerosis, 79, 80–86, 101, 103
Autonomy, 88

Baltes, P., 112
Barrier to immortality, 70
Bernard, Claude, 33
Beryllium, 88
Blaming the victim, 130

Blood lipids, 102
Blood pressure, 115
Body weight, excessive, 86
Brain size/body weight ratio, 25
Brave New World, 138
Breslow, L., 87
Build and Blood Pressure Study, 102

Calorie-deficient diet, 19
Camus, A., 126
Cancer, 64, 65, 79, 82, 83, 84, 88
    of the colon, 103
    of the liver, 82, 83, 87, 101
    of the lung, 86, 90 91, 92, 101
    metastatic, 98
    of the prostate, 85
Cannon, W. 34
Cardiac reserve, 86, 108, 110, 115, 124
Cardiovascular disease, 71, 91, 92, 98, 101,
        103, 104
Cardiovascular reserve, 116
Carrell, A., 45
Cartilage, joint, 84
Casals, P., 141
Cataract formation, 127
Cattell–Horn Figural Relations Tests, 116, 117
Cells
    cancer, 56
    intermittently dividing, 46
    postmitotic, 46
    senescence of, 45, 49, 55
    WI-38, 52
Cellular water, 36
Centenarians, 16
Cerebral hemorrhage, 81
Cerebrovascular disease, 91
Challenges, random, 99
Choice, personal, 123
Cholesterol, 81, 87
Chromate, 88
Chronic bronchitis, 101
Chronic disease, 79, 80, 93, 97, 136
    emergence of, 64, 79
    postponement of, 86, 91, 92, 105
Chronological age, 109
Churchill, W., 141
Cigarette smoking, 85, 86, 88, 90, 91, 100,
        101, 103, 105, 109, 130
Cirrhosis, 82, 83, 87, 101
Claudication, 80, 81
Clonal senescence, 47
Cockaynes' syndrome, 21
Coffee, 85

Cognitive dissonance, 119, 120
Cohort, 109, 111, 112, 114, 116
Collagen, 53
Collateral circulation, 104
Commitment theory, 52, 53
Conflict, existential, 123
Congestive heart failure, 112
Copernicus, N., 1
Coronary arteries, 103
    bypass surgery, 105
    disease, 86
Coronary care units, 105
Cross-links, collagen, 53
Cross-sectional studies, 110, 113
Cryogenics, 138
Crystallized intelligence, 116–117
Cure, 8
Curve
    bell-shaped, 71
    Gaussian, 72
    human survival, 5–7, 25, 70, 73
    rectangular, 25–40, 92, 97, 98, 121, 127,
        140
Curve-squaring technologies, 94
Cyavana, 18

Darwin, C., 1, 39
De León, Ponce, 18
"Deacon's Masterpiece, The," 135
Death
    accidental, 65, 66, 98
    pedestrian, 38
    premature, 3, 8, 59, 73, 93, 98, 101
    violent, 65, 73, 89
Death rate, age-specific, 27
Decline in infectious disease, 60
Decline, rapid, 56
Defense mechanism, 88
Dehydroepiandrosterone (DHEA), 139
Dementia, 101
Dental caries, 103
Depression, 119
Despair, 123–132
de Gaulle, C., 141
Diabetes, 63, 66, 79, 82, 83, 102
Diet, 87, 91, 100, 102, 105
Diphtheria, 62, 63
Diverticulitis, 103
DNA, 40, 54, 137
Drug compliance, 105
Drug ingestions, 100
Dubos, R., 34

Eddy, Mary Baker, 141
Einstein, A., 1
Elasticity of skin, 110, 127
Electrocardiograms, 103
Emphysema, 79, 82, 83, 86, 90, 91, 92, 101, 112
Environmental toxins, 88
Eos, 19
Epidemic, 67
Equity, social, 129
Error catastrophe theory, 54
Event-dependent, 121
Evolution, 37, 123
Exercise, 86, 91, 100–105
    aerobic, 90
    tolerance, 110

Fad diets, 100
Fasting blood glucose, 82
Fibroblasts, 46
Finch, C., 121
Fluid intelligence, 116–117
Food dyes, 88
Food restriction, 19
Fountain, myth of, 11, 18
Framingham study, 102, 103

Galen, 45
Gallbladder disease, 87
Genes, 39
Genetic code, 137
Gerovital, 18
Glucose, 86
    tolerance, 104
Gompertz, Benjamin, 27, 31, 35, 136, 147, 152
Gompertz's law, 26, 147–149
Gout, 87
Grandma Moses, 141
Graying of hair, 108, 110, 127

Hamlet, 127, 128
Hayflick, L., 46, 48, 136
Hayflick limit, 43–56
HDL cholesterol, 103, 104
Health care costs, decline, 95
Heart attack. See Cardiovascular disease
Heart output, 36
Heifetz, J., 141
Helplessness, 88
Hemorrhages, 87
Hemorrhoids, 103
Hepatitis, 101
High blood pressure, 81, 104

High-density lipoproteins, 86, 87, 102, 115
High-fiber diet, 102
Highway design, 89
Hippocrates, 44
Hippocratic tradition, 131
Hirsch, G., 55
Hodgkin's disease, 84
Holmes, Oliver Wendell, 135
Home care, 93
Homeostasis, 33–36, 98, 136
Homicide, 66, 87, 101
Hospices, 93
Human, oldest, 12
Human fibroblast cells, 46, 48
Human life, natural, 69
Human life span
    duration, 76
    ideal, 73
    maximum, 25
Humor, 119
Hunza, 13
Hutchinson–Gilford syndrome, 21
Huxley, Aldous, 19, 138
Hyperboreans, 13
Hypertension, 91, 101, 102, 103, 105
Hypertension Detection and Follow-Up
    Program, 104

Illness, premature. See Chronic disease
Immortalists, 138
Immortality, 11, 139
    barrier to, 70
    cellular, 44
Immune surveillance, 85
Industrial pollution, 85
Infections, 98
Infectious disease, decline in, 60
Infirmity, compression of, 92
Influenza, 37, 63, 98
Injury, traumatic and accidental, 89
Insulin-dependent (Type I) diabetes, 84
Insurance, medical, 129
Intelligence, crystallized and fluid, 108, 116–117
Ischemic heart disease, 104
    mortality, decline in, 105

Jared, 17
Joggers, 90, 104, 115

Kidney
    blood flow, 36
    clearance, 108

Kidney *(continued)*
    function, 110
    reserve, 127
Kramsch, D., 103

Langer, E., 118
LDL cholesterol, 103
Leaf, Alexander, 13
Left anterior descending coronary artery, 80
Life expectancy, 2, 72, 93, 94, 97
    average, 95
    change in, 74
    projected estimates of, 75
Life-extending technologies, 94
Life span, 2, 93
    finite, 25, 44, 73, 77
    maximum, 26, 30, 92, 93
    natural, 74
    prolongation of, 19
    rat, 19
Life tables, 143–146
Lifestyles, 100
Limit, Hayflick, 43–56
Liver
    cancer, 82, 83, 87, 101
    detoxification, 108
    disease, 101
Living wills, 93
Locus of control, 120
Longevity, 11
Longshoremen, 103
Lost Horizon, 13
Low-density cholesterol, 101
Low-density lipoproteins, 87, 101, 102
Low salt diet, 102
Lung cancer, 86, 90, 91, 92, 101
Lung vital capacity, 108

McKeown, T., 105
Makeham, 31, 148
Malignant cells, 45
Malignant change, 85
Malignant neoplasms, 101
Marathon, 115, 121, 124, 137
    performance, 104, 114
Marijuana, 131
Markers of aging, 107, 109, 111, 114, 124
Maximal breathing rate, 108, 110
Maximum breathing capacity, 36, 115
Maximum life potential (MLP), 3
Maximum life span, fixed, 26, 30, 92, 93
Mazess, R., 14
Measles, 62–63

Mechanisms, subcellular, 44
Medical irradiation, 88
Medical model, 2, 5
Medicine, preventive, 4
Medvedev, Zhores, 16
Memory, short-term, 108, 110
Memory tests, 118
Messenger RNA, 137
Metastatic cancer, 98
Methuselah, 11, 17, 136
    myth of, 11–23
Michelangelo, 141
Modifiable aspects of aging. *See* Plasticity
Molecular errors, 40
Morbidity, compression of, 92
Mortality, general theory of, 34
Mortality, infant, 27
Mortality curve, ideal, 71
Mortality rate, age-specific, 29, 31, 136, 145,
        148, 151
Mortality rate, exponential increase in, 29
Multiple sclerosis, 84
Muscle cells, 46
Muscular dystrophy, 84
Muscular reserve, 124

Natural death, 8, 97–105, 135, 140
    sharp downslope of, 69–77
Natural life, 97–105, 135, 140
Nerve cells, 46
Nerve conduction, 116
    velocity, 36, 108, 116
Nesselroade, J., 112
Newton, I., 1
Noah, 17
Noninsulin-dependent (Type II) diabetes, 82
Novocaine, 18

Obesity, 87, 102, 103, 130
Old age, 31
One-hoss shay, 135–142
Opacification of the lens, 110
Organ function, decline in, 31, 33
Organ reserve, 32, 80, 84, 98, 99, 101, 115,
        136, 137
    homeostasis, 33
Orgel, L., 55, 137
Osteoarthritis, 82, 83, 112, 124
Oxygen starvation, 81

Paffenbarger, R., 103, 120
Paradox, 76
Paratyphoid, 62

Paternalism, dilemma of, 131
Pedestrian, 37, 38
Personal decision making, 119
Physiological function, linear loss of, 35
Picasso, P., 141
Placebo effect, 120
Plasticity, 91, 98, 111, 124, 125
    of aging, 107–121, 125, 127
    individual, 113
    of intellectual aging, 116, 117
    maximal, 125
    of memory, 117
    physical, 114
    of social interaction, 118
Platelets, 80
Plemons, J., 116, 117
Pneumonia, 37, 63, 91, 92, 98
Polio, paralytic, 62
Polluted air, 100
Postmitotic cells, 46
Precancerous states, 82
Premature disease, elimination of, 59–67, 69
Premises, limiting, 2
Prevention, 8
Preventive medicine, 89
Progeria, 21
Protein, 40
    synthesis, 55
Psoriasis, 84
Psychological defense mechanisms, 119
Psychological health, 88
Psychological imperatives, 130
Pulmonary reserve, 86

Quality of life, 60

"Rabbi Ben Ezra," 9
Reaction time, 108, 110, 116
Rectangular curve, 25–40, 92, 97, 98, 121,
    127, 140
    implications, 70
    individual, 125
Rectangular society, 136, 139, 140–142
Rectangularization, 93, 136
Refined foods, 100
Rejuvenation, 11
Relinquishing youth, 128
Retirement, 14
    policies, 141
Retrieval cues, 118
Rheumatoid arthritis, 84
Risk factors, 89, 101, 126
RNA, 40, 54

Rothmund's syndrome, 21
Rubenstein, A., 141
Russell, Bertrand, 141
Russia, 16

Saccharin, 88
Sacher, G., 39
Saturated fats, 90
Schaie, K. W., 112
Schizophrenia, 84
Schweitzer, Albert, 141
Seat belts, 89
Selection, natural, 44, 100
Self-care movement, 4
Self-worth, 88
Seligman, M., 88, 119
Semantics, 8
Senescence, 4, 43, 98, 99, 100, 107, 114, 115,
    128
    cell, 45, 49, 55
Serum cholesterol, 86, 103, 115
Shangri-La, 11, 13, 136
Shaw, George Bernard, 17, 141
Shock, Nathan, 31, 137
Short-term memory, 108, 110
Sisyphus, 121, 126
Skiing, 104
Skin elasticity, 108
Smallpox, 62–63
Smog, 87
Social interaction, plasticity of, 118
Social isolation, 118
Society, ideal, 93
Society, rectangular, 136, 139, 140–142
Somatic cells, 46, 56
Special-interest lobbies, 90
Species life span, maximum, 26, 30, 92, 93
Speed limits, 89
Spiral, cost, 7
Spirduso, W., 116
Strehler, B., 34, 136
Strehler–Mildvan theory, 151–152
Streptococcal, 62, 63
Streptomycin, 61
Stroke, 81, 91, 92
Suicide, 63, 66, 87, 101, 127, 128
Super-centenarian, 11, 12, 136
Superlongevity, 138, 139
Suppression, 88, 119
Survival curves, human, 5–7, 25. See also
        Rectangular curve
    ideal, 73
    sequential, 70

Syllogism, new, 1–9
Symptomatic threshold, 85
Syphilis, 62, 63

Terminal collapse, 135
Terminal drop, 121, 127, 128
Tetanus, 62
Thinning of hair, 127
Thomas, Dylan, 9
Thomas, Lewis, 23, 135
Threshold, clinical, 86
Thrombosis, 80
Time stresses, 100
Tissue culture studies, 46
Tithonus, 19
Tobacco crops, 89, 90
Tortoises, Galapagos, 51
Totman, R., 120
Toxic chemicals, 90
Transient ischemic attacks, 81
Trauma, 73
Trauma bump, 27
Triumph, 123–132
Tuberculosis, 60, 61, 63

Typhoid fever, 62–63

Ulcerative colitis, 84
Universal chronic disease, 80–85
    decrease in, 111

VA Cooperative Study, 104
Vakutia, 16
Valliant, G., 87, 88, 119
Variability, 108, 111, 115
Veatch, R., 130
Vilcabamba, 13, 14
Vitality, 9, 35
Vitamin E, 18

Weight Watchers, 130
Wells, H. G. 138
Werner's syndrome, 21
Whooping cough, 62–63
Wilde, Oscar, 19
Wisdom of the body, 34
"Wonderful One-Hoss Shay," 135

Zorba the Greek, 141